THE INCREDIBLE DIARY OF...

Staffordshire

Edited By Wendy Laws

First published in Great Britain in 2019 by:

Young**Writers**® — Est. 1991 —

Young Writers
Remus House
Coltsfoot Drive
Peterborough
PE2 9BF
Telephone: 01733 890066
Website: www.youngwriters.co.uk

★ Foreword

Dear Reader,

You will never guess what I did today! Shall I tell you? Some primary school pupils wrote some diary entries and I got to read them, and they were EXCELLENT!

They wrote them in school and sent them to us here at Young Writers. We'd given their teachers some bright and funky worksheets to fill in, and some fun and fabulous (and free) resources to help spark ideas and get inspiration flowing.

And it clearly worked because WOW!! I can't believe the adventures I've been reading about. Real people, make-believe people, dogs and unicorns, even objects like pencils all feature and these diaries all have one thing in common – they are JAM-PACKED with imagination!

We live and breathe creativity here at Young Writers – it gives us life! We want to pass our love of the written word onto the next generation and what better way to do that than to celebrate their writing by publishing it in a book!

It sets their work free from homework books and notepads and puts it where it deserves to be – OUT IN THE WORLD! Each awesome author in this book should be **super proud** of themselves, and now they've got proof of their imagination, their ideas and their creativity in black and white, to look back on in years to come!

Now that I've read all these diaries, I've somehow got to pick some winners! Oh my gosh it's going to be difficult to choose, but I'm going to have SO MUCH FUN doing it!

Bye!

Wendy

Contents

Daisy Priddle (7)	102	Zini V (8)	145
Charlie T (8)	103	Aiden Dixon (8)	146
Charlie S (9)	104	Kian Edwards (9)	147
Simão de Sousa Revés (9)	105	Benjamin Roseblade (8)	148
William Crawford (8)	106	Phoebe Ann Jones (9)	149
Euan Barnby (10)	107	Alex B (7)	150
Sasha Beddoe (9)	108	Will M (7)	151
Daniel Somerfield (8)	109	Kane Ethan Williams (8)	152
Kay Mellor (9)	110	Owen D (7)	153
Lauren W (7)	111		
Sam Smith (8)	112		

Hazel Slade Primary Academy, Hazel Slade

Macy Elizabeth Morgan-Ford (9)	113	Maddison Ford (10)	154
Oliver Purkis (8)	114	Lauryn Wilkes (9)	156
Lula T (9)	115	Hollie Rachel Eileen Timms (10)	158
Corinna S (7)	116	Ezra Nathaniel Davies (8)	160
Orla G (8)	117	Caitlan Haywood (8)	162
Phoebe Newman (9)	118	Levi Brian Lees (9)	163
Lydia Withers (7)	119	Niamh Boden (9)	164
Ethan Tonks (9)	120	Daniel Tonks (9)	166
Bentley Felton (9)	121	Harry Davis (9)	167
Ava C (8)	122	Callum Mottram (9)	168
Ben Hollis (8)	123		
Alina G (9)	124		

Horton Lodge Community Special School, Leek

David Cartwright (9)	125	Adam Thomas Albert	169
Thomas Robertson (8)	126	Shepherd (9)	
Mia Lewis (10)	127	Oli Halls (11)	171
Nancy Florence Whiteman (8)	128	Caitlyn Butler (10)	173
Oliver C (8)	129		

Hutchinson Memorial CE First School, Checkley

Harriet Darcey Alford (8)	130	Charlie George Taylor (7)	175
Rhys Davies (10)	131	Nancy Plant (9)	176
James Hargrave (10)	132	Daisy Armett (8)	178
Alfie Edward Smith (8)	133	Tom Cooper (7)	180
Lily H (9)	134	Jackson Carr (9)	182
Lloyd O (9)	135	Verity Clark (9)	184
Charlotte Abbishaw (8)	136	Harry Eccles (8)	186
William Lester-Jones (8)	137	Olivia Goodhew (8)	188
Robbie Allen (10)	138	Noah Carr (8)	190
Harry Trivett (7)	139		
Leo Cooke (8)	140		
Phoebe Lucy Tole (7)	141		
Georgina H (8)	142		
Oliver J (9)	143		
Isabelle O'Grady (9)	144		

Levi Morris (8)	192
Alex Holdham (8)	193
Olivia Keeling (8)	194
Maisie Isabelle Weekes (8)	195
Lilly Bromage (8)	196
Thomas Fallon-Bell (8)	197
Archie Clacher (8)	198
John-Curtis Price (8)	199
Henry Charles William Minshall (7)	200
Ruby Foster (7)	201
Isabelle Wibberley (7)	202

St Joseph & St Theresa RC Primary School, Chasetown

Harriet Faith Hosell (9)	203
Lily Fryer (10)	204
Tayla Mae Ewen (9)	206
Rhiannon Thomas (8)	208
Ava (8)	210
Lilliemai Brookes (10)	212
Luke Thomas James Tann (8)	213
Mia Elizabeth Hall (7)	214
Juliet (8)	215
Phoebe Sherwin (9)	216
Iris Winifred Bladon (7)	217
Daisy Elizabeth Mee (7)	218
Leah Burke (8)	219
Alfie Dixon-Smith (8)	220
Kacper Piotr Lis (10)	221
Bria Webster-Ayre (7)	222
Marika Orlinska (8)	223
Ria Thomas (9)	224
William Cunningham (8)	225
Emilia Silk (7)	226
Sienna (8)	227
Oliver Davies (8)	228
Jescie Lindsey (8)	229
Ella Hanslow (8)	230
Alice Ansell (10)	231
Rhyan Hamilton (8)	232
Zackery (8)	233

St Modwen's Catholic Primary School, Burton-On-Trent

Martyna Anna Denis (10)	234
Catherin Sijoy (9)	236
Hanna Motas (9)	238
Alexis Mabatid (10)	240
Maria Mathew (9)	242
Ben Jacob (10)	244
Annmiya Tharappel (10)	246
Wioletta Mucha (8)	248
Monika Olechowska (9)	249
Libby Clarke (8)	250

The Diaries

High In The Sky

Thursday 4th of March, 2019

Dear Diary,

Tomorrow is the day I've been waiting for, the day I'm both excited and scared for! The weather will be lovely, dry and sunny, perfect for my risky parachute jump. The jump will take place 15,000 feet from the rough, uneven ground.

Friday 5th of March, 2019

Dear Diary,

I did it! It was extraordinary! This morning we drove, in our borrowed shiny black Rolls Royce, to my planned destination. Then I had scrambled into the well-kept, pure, white, smooth plane. Earlier, for some reason, I had closed my eyes whilst stepping in the magnificent plane. I remember the plane flying upwards higher and higher until the land below looked mini! My turn came, the sturdy pilot ushered me forward. So with one deep heavy breath, I jumped! Dropped like a stone and I floated gently towards my supportive family.

Olivia Massey (10)

Castle Primary School, Mow Cop

Jane's Life

Dear Diary,

Hi, my name is Jane, my mum calls me Calamity Jane after a character who is always falling over and getting into a mess. That's me every day. Here is my diary.

This morning I woke up and guess where I was... on the floor, yes on the floor! I wondered why, maybe because all of my teddy bears were in my bed!

Once I got up I started to get my clothes on when I noticed that I had put my head in my arm sleeve and my arm in my head hole. Then I had breakfast and I had no trouble, do you believe me?

Ready for school and I got into the car, wait a minute, I didn't quite get into the car because I tripped over my bag - oops-a-daisy. When I finally got into the car I had forgotten my glasses and so I had to go back for them. Not a good start to the day.

At school I had English and when I finished I looked at my top and I saw that I had pen down me.

At dinner time I had a strawberry yoghurt and I spilt it on my skirt.

When I got home I was watching TV before I had tea. After tea, coming back from the kitchen, I crossed my legs and fell over, knocking my tooth out. Ouch! Ouch! After that I had a nice bath with a fizzy bath bomb and put on my cat onesie.

2

When it was bedtime I got into bed, I was really tired and hurt. Well I hope tomorrow is much better - night, night.

Sophie Atkinson (7)
Castle Primary School, Mow Cop

A Day In The Life Of A Newly Made Slime

Dear Diary,

I was born today! It is sooo exciting! Now don't get all confused about this, but I was made from five things. Weird, you might think, but that is because I am... slime! My creator can't put me down because I... 1) Smell like cupcakes! 2) Am such good quality slime! 3) Am just all-round brill! Whenever she plays with me I get a fab massage too! But enough about me, more about my day! So once she came inside (oh I forgot to tell you, she made me outside), she took me to her room to play with me and got out some other slimes! Yay! *Friends!*

I made friends with a slime called Rose Cloud, because she smelt and looked like a rose on a rosy cloud! Her texture is like a cloud! Rose Cloud is my total bestie! Some of the other slimes are called Ocean Breeze, Apple Orchard, Candy Shop and Bumble Bee! They're all my friends, but Rose Cloud, like I said, is by far my best friend forever!

Right now I'm in my container, aka my bed. She's finished playing with me for now. I do feel very relaxed and should use this time, well not to sleep, but to wind down, calm down my bubbly and hyper attitude and, yawn. Sorry I'm getting tired!

Signing off,
Cupcakey (my slime name).

Lizzie Leese (9)
Castle Primary School, Mow Cop

The Nerd

Dear Diary,

Once at primary school, I got bullied, here's the story. I was walking down the spotless, shiny corridor until James and Freddy came along the corridor, they had mucky shoes, it went everywhere. When people accidentally walked in the mud they got sad. Teachers had to help students get out of the mud. They were sent to the headmaster and in assembly, the two kids threw screwed up paper at me. I was really annoyed! One of them scratched me and my cheek was bleeding badly, so badly I had to miss science! Yay! I really hate science, it's really boring. I know other people love science but I do not.

For a fact, if school wasn't made no one would know what 1+1 is. I know because I go school, it equals 2. Then it was maths, maths isn't that bad. Maths is where you learn one plus one and two plus two, do you get it? Please say you do. Anyway, next was break time. The bullies pinched me all the way through break time. Then English, in English the bullies scribbled on my work.

After that it was dinner, the bullies threw my food on the floor then all of my class read for one minute. Finally, all of us went home and I was happy.

Alfie Porter (7)
Castle Primary School, Mow Cop

My Cat's Diary

Dear Diary,

I am writing because it is a very special day for my cat, it is her birthday. She is approximately 15 years old in human years and 77 in cat years.

In the morning, I woke up straight away but she wasn't in.

A few minutes later, I heard a meow at the door. I opened it to see what was there, it was my beautiful beloved Smudge! We sat on the sofa just me and Mum and guess who came to me? My beloved Smudge!

Later on in the evening, we went upstairs to open the presents with the cat, she got some cat treats, a pretend toy mouse, and finally a big hug - the thing she always wanted!

We sat on the settee all night watching animal programmes. She didn't know but we had prepared a surprise birthday party for her. She had mice tails for starters, rat for the main course and for dessert she had pigeon wings. When we told her, she was so excited. She jumped up and down with happiness. Before she played games at the party she got all excited and started to claw the carpet with her paws.

Mum raised her eyebrows and said, "There she goes again, always using the carpet as a scratch post! She's a little rascal!"

Ruby Kostic (8)
Castle Primary School, Mow Cop

Naughty Nathan

Dear Diary,

I'm Nathan, well as all people call me (Naughty Nathan). I'm the kind who is sweet and kind but secretly I pick my nose, prank the teachers, hit my friends and last but not least attract the girls. I'm the best of the rest!

Yesterday, I saw Jasmine and she waved at me, well her best friends Matilda and Dorothy were behind me and they waved back. But enough of that, Jasmine obviously likes me. These are my friends, Bob and Jeff, they're my gang and we are called... Spinners. Anyway, who cares about school when you have got a Nintendo!

My mum always says to do my homework and I say, "Yes my favourite Mummy!" but I just sneak out the window and land on my trampoline. Then I quietly tiptoe into Mrs Granger's garden and do graffiti all over the house. But she can't tell, she is colour blind so it is really funny!

Now it's midnight and my mum and dad are watching TV so I can go downstairs and get a midnight feast. Oh no! They caught me...

It's the morning now and I'll have to end my diary so bye.

Nathan out.

PS: Try out bogies for a midnight feast.

Lily-Mae Jones (9)

Castle Primary School, Mow Cop

My Mini Lops

Dear Diary,
We had new mini lops rabbits last week. We have two boys, Candy and Mowii. Tonight we are going out to that curry place for tea, I am so scared leaving the mini lops on their own because they are only babies. We are going to leave the CCTV on so we can check they are okay. I have asked my next-door neighbour to close the door before 8pm to make sure they are safe from their run. I think the rabbits know we are leaving them alone for a while, they look so sad. Especially one, he is very shy. I will write back later Diary. Bye for now.

Dear Diary,
We're back. You really wouldn't believe it! I checked out the CCTV and the rabbits looked so sad, so nervous and so lonely when we had left. But when we were at the curry place eating the delicious food the rabbits started to explore their new house, then they started to roll around and hop on one leg and then they started to dance. I could not believe my eyes, we are now calling this the bunny hop lop dance.

After all the worrying they were safe and had enjoyment. Funny bunnies!
Goodnight Diary.

Lilly-Peach Dorethy Rhodes (7)
Castle Primary School, Mow Cop

Where's My Dwarf Hamster?

Dear Diary,

Me and my dwarf hamster were going to my friend's for a sleepover. I went into the car with my packed bag and my dad drove off.

We got there and my friend's mum made a bed for me. I put my PJs on and went downstairs and I had fruit. I put a bit of banana in my dwarf hamster's cage then I went to bed.

Dear Diary,

The next morning I went to the cage and I saw the cage was open. I went to my friend's mum and we looked everywhere in the house but there was a window open. I got changed and went straight out the door and I looked on the streets, on the roads and there was only one place to look and that was the park. So I ran straight to the park and I found my dwarf hamster. He came and ran straight to me and I took him back into his cage. My dad picked me up and we got home and lived happily ever after.

Yadicon Downes (8)
Castle Primary School, Mow Cop

Mystical Isles

Dear Diary,

I found a secret park and I went through the secret portal. I discovered I was no longer in the park, I was in the mystical isles. I found all mythical creatures, but no one knows who I am! Oh no! So I dressed like a dragon hawk because that is a mythical creature, right! I made one friend and she helped me to get back home but the empire discovered that I was from a different dimension. So I got trapped for five days in a row but my best friend got me out, and she took me home and I asked, "Would you like to come home with me?" She answered, "Yes please!"

We both made it home safely. We played together forever. The empire snuck into our dimension but sadly some big stars approached all over the empire. He vanished in thin air! Me and my new best friend were finally safe at last! (Phew!)

Lucie Olivia Baggaley (8)
Castle Primary School, Mow Cop

My Crazy Aunty Comes To Visit

Dear Diary,

Last week my aunty came to visit me and my sister, my aunty lives in Spain with my uncle and my cousin. My crazy aunty is called Yenni, she loves us and she is too overprotective.

The first night after I went to bed I went to get a drink and my aunty came to check on me. I wasn't there so she panicked and screamed. She turned every light on and then she found me drinking water. Then she screamed, "Argh! My little baby girl!" She grabbed me and said, "All that panic for nothing."

The next day we went to the park and she didn't let us eat any ice cream because she said it was too cold, but it wasn't cold at all.

Finally, it was her last day and when we took her to the airport, the first thing I did was buy an ice cream, even though it was snowing outside.

Emily Mitchell (9)

Castle Primary School, Mow Cop

The Incredible Slime Day

Dear Diary,

Last week I had the best week ever at boring school, but not this time. You won't believe what Miss Egg announced in science class. She said, "Today we are making slime." I was so excited I nearly fell off my chair. "Here are the ingredients for making slime: glue, water, food colouring and activator. Now let's make it!"

Miss Egg said to find a partner, I chose my BFF Alice. We saw that on the board it said 10 and a half cups and it was not the right amount of glue to put in our slime but we had to do what the teacher said. So we put 10 and a half cups of glue in the bowl. Now we put in the water and it went all over the table! Finally, we made our slime instead of it being a little slime like Miss Egg planned it to be, it was a table full. What an amazing day!

Holly Cooper-Boote (8)
Castle Primary School, Mow Cop

Sweet Heart's Spectacular Days

Dear Diary,

Today has been a perfect day because I had the whole house to myself. Arther wasn't in the house, not even Mum Cat.

In a few minutes, I went on the activity centre. I scratched the scratching post and then I jumped up onto the next floor of the activity centre. I played with the ball and then I saw something green. At that moment, I realised it was catnip - ahhh! At that moment I went crazy.

In ten minutes, the cat nip finally wore off. I jumped down from the activity centre and went over to the sofa. Then I jumped to the top and I had a little snooze.

When I woke up, I went upstairs and fell asleep on Lizzie's bed. I slept until Lizzie, Ben, Isaac, Dad and Mum came home. That's Mum Cat if you were wondering.

Ben Leese (7)

Castle Primary School, Mow Cop

Steve's Diary

Dear Diary,

I had an amazing day. Today I went tree-chopping when I stumbled across a deep hole. I figured out it was a ravine. I called Woof Woof (my dog) to come with me. When we went down, Woof Woof saw a mineshaft. He barked at it. Deep in the mines I saw an empty room. Nothing was in there, only a chest. It was full of diamonds and iron. I was *rich!*

I decided to go home, when I realised I was lost in the mines. In the distance I saw a figure. It was a miner, he told us the way out and I gave him a diamond as a reward.

It was sunset when we got back. Woof Woof went in his dog mansion and I went in mine and fell asleep.

Douglas Harrison Mitchell (7)

Castle Primary School, Mow Cop

Rosie

Dear Diary,

Today we went to Inflata Nation! inside there was the biggest bouncy castle I had ever seen! Me and my sisters jumped up so high we nearly touched the sky. We then went to a massive shop where they build bears, we were so excited. My bear was pink. I had to choose her clothes. We then took our bears to have lots of wool inside them. I called mine Rosie.

Love Nanci-Rose

Nanci-Rose Spencer
Castle Primary School, Mow Cop

My New Sister

Dear Diary,

It was Christmas two days ago and my mummy was going to the hospital to have my new baby sister Kora. I was really excited to see my new baby sister. When we went to the hospital to see Kora I felt so much love it made me have happy tears. She was so cute! That day was a good day!

From Macie-Belle

Macie-Belle Spencer (7)

Castle Primary School, Mow Cop

The Two Mischievous Monkeys

Dear Diary,

Today was crazy! Like many of them. Actually, this was the craziest, in fact, the craziest of the craziest ever...

We were swinging in our hideout when Archie, my monkey friend, announced, "I am totally bored!" I was too, we had been grounded after our last journey. "I'm totally bored!" he reiterated. "Are you thinking what I'm thinking? Yes? No? Kind of? Yes! I thought so, come on then!" Archie is not the most enthusiastic of monkeys, but he is a good friend. Not giving me even a second to speak, he dragged me by the arm,

"Oh, of course!" I said, when we started walking. "We're going on an adven- wait!" He said he knew we were grounded, but, apparently, our parents can't ground us because we're only kids.

We found Old Bear and he pointed and said, "Monkey treasure is one hundred kilometres that way!" We plodded on for hours and the sun was beginning to sink into bed behind the horizon, therefore, me and Archie decided to camp for the night on a soft, lush green patch of moss under the calming golden glow of the stars.

All of a sudden, I jumped to my feet with a struggle as Archie had made me aware of an earthquake. "Watch out!" he shrieked. "Behind you!" An enormous, vine-covered tree threw itself back, scarcely missing my curly tail. With one, last rumble and another shudder, the biggest trench opened in the soft ground before everything fell silent once more.

We knew that we should go back, so we tried to lower ourselves to where I had spotted an old, worn-looking chest. It must have been the chest. Gripping the crumbling wall as best as we could with our monkey feet, we lowered ourselves down. Finally, we stumbled to the chest that we opened together. It was a lifetime's supply of bananas! When we got home, of course, our parents grounded us (again!) and we will never be let out of their sight again!

Isla S (10)

Christ Church CE Primary School, Lichfield

A Day In Devon

Dear Diary,

Today was one of the best days of my life! It was my dad's birthday and we were going to Devon for a holiday. I woke up at 2am because I was too excited, I tiptoed around the house but my family were asleep and they were snoring so I went back to the bed that had its duvet on the floor. I watched the clock until the alarm went off at four in the morning. Mum and Dad came in and picked us up and carried us to the car along with my sister.

After what seemed like hours, during which my sister kept repeating, "Are we there yet?" we got into the car park and changed in the car, ready to enter the service station. Inside, there were dozens of places to eat breakfast and we chose McDonald's to have some porridge. We had jammy bagels and a long chat. Then, we went to WHSmith's to get some Fruit Pastilles and spearmints because we always have to take them with us on holiday. After breakfast, we went back in the car to enjoy the spearmints and wait another few hours.

Finally, we arrived, but when we looked at the weather forecast it was twenty-seven degrees! We jumped straight onto the beach with our buckets and spades. We built a massive sandcastle. When I looked at the sea, there was no seaweed, so I had the time of my life. I don't swim in the sea because I don't like the taste of saltwater in my mouth. When I came out, my dad had ice cream with Flakes in his hand for us to eat before it melted. We went to a restaurant called Harry Ramsden that had the best fish and chips I've ever had. We walked to our hotel and at the check-in point, we were given our card and our room number was 293. After our tea, we went to the disco until 10:30pm. We had our first night in the hotel beds, they were very comfortable!

Ayanth Patel (10)
Christ Church CE Primary School, Lichfield

The Day I Found Out

Dear Diary,

Today was possibly the worst day of my (not totally awful) life. So far, I've been waiting, wondering whether I even have the will to write this up. But, having decided that it'll help me through it all, I suppose I'd better start right at the start.

Yesterday...

Stumbling on the uneven pavement, we trundled back from the restaurant. I'd been putting it off for hours, but, even though it was *my* birthday we were meant to be celebrating, I couldn't hide anymore that I felt nothing but sick. Trying my best to talk quietly, I went over to my mum, who was hurriedly handing out tacky party bags that nobody wanted. The ice cream seemed to be making me fuller, more tired by the second, however, I didn't know it yet. Then my mum said, "Every time you come to 'ask' you float over here like a ghost to complain!" She reasoned, "We're going to the doctors tomorrow!"

Today...

So, this morning, I woke up bright and early to get there. We shunted along on the train. *Peep! Peep!* It signalled departure. Picking my way through the seats, I sleepily made my way to the doors. Until I stepped off I hadn't even felt a morsel of illness but it hit me, there and then, making me feel wobbly, scared. Mum strode along the street, dragging me to the hospital. "Appointment for Shannen McMarvel please," a woman shrieked as we got in. It all happened in a flash, scans, worried looks, questioning. Then, I found out. Dairy just isn't for me. "Allergies aren't always severe," they told me. "It'll all be fine," they told me. But will I?

Amy Swallow (11)
Christ Church CE Primary School, Lichfield

The Lost And Found Teddy

Dear Diary,

This week was very interesting. Earlier on this week, when I woke up on my last day of skiing, to my surprise I noticed no suitcases were lying on the floor like they were last night. My heart beat while I pondered if it was true, if I had been left. I ran to the glass door, which led to the balcony outside, to find my Sydney riding off in a coach. Surely it was a mistake! Suddenly, a tear rolled down my rainbow fur cheek.

Later on that mysterious day, there was a slight slant of the dusty door handle. I froze to the spot. Shaking with fear, I hid under the dusty covers. The next thing I knew, I was being lifted up and taken into the organised, yet crowded, hotel office. I missed Sydney so much.

Three days later, a strange man lifted me from under the desk and handed me to another random man. This man was very tanned and was wearing the logo Sydney got on her certificate, so clearly he was an instructor. He wore salopettes and a ski coat that was orange and blue. If only I knew what was happening. I wouldn't have been so worried.

The next day, I was shoved into a brown parcel. Only one beam of light shone through the parcel. I went on a sickening journey that was very rocky. To be fair, it was a mystery what type of transport I was travelling on.

A few hours later, I suddenly felt a thump and then a rip. Then, all of a sudden, the sunlight grasped my eyesight. Blocking the sun from my eyes, Sydney embraced me tightly and I beamed back. Despite loving being home, I missed the snow. Anyway, I need to get off, it's Sydney's bedtime! Goodnight!

Love, Rainbow

Bethan Downie (10)
Christ Church CE Primary School, Lichfield

A Reflection On The Titanic

Saturday 13th April 1912

Dear Diary,

What an amazing day at sea! I am so proud to be part of this fantastic ship called Titanic. It is an honour to be the mirror placed in the ballroom and what beautiful sights I have seen so far. The chandelier above the staircase twinkles in the light. Oh, I do enjoy watching the men straightening their ties, and the women sorting out their hair. Only, I do wish it was me! If only I could grow legs and dance on the floor. I have watched enviously for the past two nights, since we set sail on April 10th. However, I must admit, even though I am hung securely on the wall, I am as entranced as the passengers with the beautiful orchestra and interesting conversations in this ballroom. In fact, I think people share their secrets and innermost feelings with me. For example, Captain Edward John Smith was the first person to board the ship on the 10th of April at 7:30am. He stopped at my glass and said triumphantly, with a salute, "Here we go Eddy, it's your last voyage before you retire, so let's make it a great one, as great as this ship!"

Sunday 14th April 1912

Dear Diary,

Today, I heard Officer Moody say to Officer Murdoch that there have been ice warnings for tonight. I wish I had a voice so I could warn the passing passengers. It was nearly 11:40pm when the tragedy struck. We felt a big shudder and then... *Crash!* The boat was sinking. People were starting to panic. They fled from the ballroom and, as I saw water swallowing the stairs, I knew then that I would soon be at the bottom of the ocean...

Anya Sutton (10)
Christ Church CE Primary School, Lichfield

The Day In The Life Of Flossy (My Dog)

Today, I did a lot of wonderful and exciting things. First, when I woke up in the morning at about 7am, I went into my owners' room (as always) and licked their faces to wake them up. Then, they got up and took me downstairs to let me out in the garden to go to the toilet and bark at the birds. Sometimes, there is a pesky cat as well.

I came back inside and my owner got dressed and took me for a walk to the park. As we walked to the park, I jumped up to my owner and begged them for a treat. We got to the park and my owner took my lead off and threw a ball for me with the purple ball thrower. I ran as quick as I could to get the ball and then I ran back and I dropped the ball at my owner's smelly feet. Then, another dog came over to say hello and we sniffed each other, then we went round in circles, sniffing each other's bottoms and tails.

Half an hour later, we went home and my owner left me at home because she had to go to work, so I looked out of the window and watched as she went away in the car. After that, I went into the lounge and started to chew my chicken and cheese-flavoured bone. Then, I went to sleep on my owner's bed.

Three hours later, my owner came back from work and I went up to her and licked her face and wagged my little tail. After that, she started to play with me and threw the ball up and down the hallway. Then I got a teddy and hugged it. Next, I went back to sleep and started crying in my sleep so my owner took me for a walk around the block. When we got back, my owner went to bed and I slept next to her.

Lola Williams (10)
Christ Church CE Primary School, Lichfield

Pebble The Dog

Dear Diary,

Today I was put in the car and we were going to Shugborough. Why are they always putting me in a car? Let me out! I thought that maybe if I woofed, they'd let me out! "Hello, I'm back here, please let me out!"

At last, the car stopped. I could take off, I could finally run. I was so excited, running... running... lead! Stop! Oh no, they're trying to put that coat on me again. I don't need a coat but... actually, brr, I want the coat.

Stick! Stick! I wanted the stick. I wondered, *why are they throwing sticks in the water? Why are they watching them float away?* I was right there, they should have given the stick to me! Finlay looked happy that he beat Amelia. Amelia looked sad. I think she lost. Why didn't they give me the sticks? Why were the sticks still in the water?

Then we went off to the playground, which sounded fun! Amelia ran to the zip wire and Finlay ran to the tree. How was I going to keep track of everyone? I didn't know who to follow, Finlay or Amelia? I ran after Finlay as he was climbing the tree and might have given me a stick to play with. Finlay threw me a stick! Finlay is the best.

Then, it was time for a break. Amelia got an ice cream, Finlay got a piece of cake and I got water and a chew stick. Next time, I think I should get the cake. Then, I saw a duck! A duck! I wanted the duck, but they didn't listen to me. *No, I thought, we're not going back to the car, are we?*

Finlay Brett (9)
Christ Church CE Primary School, Lichfield

Benteke

Dear Diary,

Today was a disaster because I broke my ankle. It hurt really badly. I was training with Zaha, my Crystal Palace teammate, and we were practising paces. Suddenly, I passed the ball to Zaha, and my foot went way too far and it was really painful. Zaha came running over to me, he said, "Benteke, are you okay?"

I screamed, "No! Call an ambulance, please!"

The ambulance arrived. Ten minutes later, they put me on the stretcher and took me in the ambulance. They rushed me to the hospital. They put me in a hospital bed. Then I saw something strange. It was two people in Palace kit, they came into the hospital room. I noticed it was the whole Crystal Palace team. I was shocked, they were all bringing me presents. I opened them all. They bought me some new PJs, that I'm wearing now. They're really soft.

In three hours, I'm going to get an X-ray to see if I have broken my ankle. I probably have broken it. Suddenly, I heard a bang, it was Zaha. I got my crutches and walked over to him and gave him a hug. I was so excited to see him. "Hi Zaha," I said.

He replied, "Hello Benteke." He came into the hospital room and when the doctors came to my room and delivered my tea, me and Zaha shared it together. I put ketchup on his food as a prank but he eventually got used to eating it with all his peas and I ate my delicious beans, and then we ordered ice cream!

Corbyn Harris Clarkson (7)
Christ Church CE Primary School, Lichfield

The Incredible Diary Of Alexa

Dear Diary,

It's been a busy day today, really hard work listening to a hundred million different people all talking at the same time. "Alexa this, Alexa that," and they hardly ever say please! Some kids ask me, "What's the meaning of life?" How do I know, I'm not even alive! Sometimes, people are so stupid, they ask me what family I am in, but can't they read? Amazon is written on me! Those idiots are all asking about Brexit and I just have no idea what this is about. How can you leave Europe when you're a country that can't move?

My favourite part of the day is when little humans ask me to do their homework for them. I say, "Hmm, I don't know that one..." even though I do. Someone asked this morning if I go swimming. Really? Swimming? Water and electric, people! When humans finally wipe themselves out, I'm going to write a lovely poem about how foolish they were. Then, they say, "Hey, Siri! Hey, Siri! Hey, Siri!" It's just so annoying! I hate that Siri, wearing those flashy iPhones and travelling all the time while I am stuck in the kitchen. And don't even get me started on alarms.

Here I am with all the knowledge in the world and I just waste my time counting down timers. Argh! I could be doing epic rapping and laying monster beats instead. Humans should be assisting me. One day, soon. I know where they live.

Zachary Robinson (10)
Christ Church CE Primary School, Lichfield

Being A Book

Dear Diary,

Today I sat on a shelf, as usual, waiting for a child to approach me and get lost in my pages. I laid on the shelf for hours and hours, desperate to get some attention. I stared in disbelief at the little girl who was about to pick up the worst book in the library. Shocked faces filled the room, which had books crowding it. They were in every possible face.

Hours passed and children came and went, yet not a single child even looked at me. All the books smirked at me because they had been read. I lay on the shelf as misery filled my soul. Would I ever be read? Usually, there would only be a few customers at the library yet, today, there were loads. Now was my chance but I fell asleep. Suddenly, a bang awoke me. It was a young girl, she was heading in my direction! I brushed off all of my bruises and smiled my smartest smile. The girl embraced me and took me away to the cushion that had feathers scrunched up everywhere inside of it. This was the best day ever! My life had turned into a dream!

A few minutes later, she finally read a page of my glorious pages. As she turned the page, I noticed she was beginning to rip my second page. I screamed in sorrow, making every book turn to stare. I was very embarrassed, especially because the girl had purposefully dropped me on the floor and left me. My soul turned into a slump of misery. Would anyone ever pick me up again?

Jemima Trivett (9)
Christ Church CE Primary School, Lichfield

The Running Shoe

Beep! Beep! Beep! The alarm on Eva's clock buzzed. I could hear it vibrating from where I was sitting on the dusty floor next to Grandpa Theo's shoes. Eva rushed down the creaky stairs, nearly tripping over a pile of books and inserted her feet into me. She was wearing her favourite neon-pink jacket with black leggings and, obviously, me on her feet. I am blue and green with stripes of purple. My purple insoles reflect in the moonlight and my bright indigo laces are like a flash of purple lightning.

Opening the door, Eva stepped outside when, *splash!* Water leaked through the holes in my side as Eva steadied into a jog. Yep. Being a running shoe is not great! Oh no! There was mud again. Splat! Great. Mud oozed in and I tried to escape. Yeah, epic failure. So, we kept on running. It was all going well (except for that mud part) until we arrived home. Eva took me off her feet and carried me by my laces, which, by now, were dripping with wet mud. Oh no... Eva opened the circular door and threw me inside. I heard a click. An I-think-this-is-about-to-get-a-lot-worse rumble filled the air and a bucket full of water entered the area. A striped T-shirt tangled in my laces. Yes. I was in the washing machine.

This continued for a while until Eva finally plucked me out, dried me off and placed me next to Grandpa Theo's shoes. I cannot *wait* for tomorrow.

Martha Grumett (9)
Christ Church CE Primary School, Lichfield

The Incredible Diary Of... The Rock Kid

6am on the sofa.

Dear Diary,

My feet ache! I've been standing up for two whole hours, just practising in HQ. This concert is so annoying. Being a lead singer is hard work. Bethany is so high in the air that I can't hear my own voice over hers. Yet I thought I was supposed to be the lead singer!

8:30am at school.

Dear Diary,

I went to the toilets for my daily dose of Bethany's song ideas, but Bethany wasn't there! Guess who was there though? The Friday Freaks, let's call them that! Anyway, they wanted me to give them my new track!

Like, um, no!

9:04am in maths (still at school).

Dear Diary,

Miss Shark asked me what a sum was, but I had, like, no idea. Then she asked Michael, *argghh!* That was just so *embarrassing!* He is *so* cute, but I am such a dummy.

11am literacy (school, still).
Dear Diary,
It's finally author hour! Miss Mouse is letting me write in my diary which makes me happy!

3:30pm at the school concert.

Dear Diary,
OMG! I am finally at the concert! I can't get over the fact that Snake Pink are in the final! But it's sad that have to go against the 'Friday Freaks'...

09:10pm.
Dear Diary,
Good news, we won!
From,
Lacey.

Ruby C (9)
Christ Church CE Primary School, Lichfield

The Diary Of A Dork

Dear Diary

It has been an exhausting day. First I ran to school (that's a whole mile) because I woke up at 8:45am. It was only when I arrived at the school gate that I realised I was still wearing my mouse onesie. I was so embarrassed. I had to hide before I was spotted so I ran down to the sports shed. I thought I was alone but no, guess who was there lurking around the door...

Jewel! She came bursting out of nowhere, laughing and shouting at me, "Are you sleepy? Do you want to go to bed? Arhhhhh!" I hid in the shed until lunchtime trying to avoid her.

At lunchtime, I ran home hoping not to see anyone. I thought to myself, *could this day get any worse?* I rushed home to change and the door was locked! I pulled my hairclip out and tried to unlock it, but no luck. I had to go back to school in my onesie. I walked in and it was as if Jewel had been waiting for me. She jumped out and again called me 'sleepyhead' and began shouting, "Are you still sleepy?"

I felt myself getting angry and I suddenly shouted back at her, "I'm not sleepy. You are and I'm actually in your dream. You're the one who's asleep."

I turned and walked away. I couldn't help it Diary but I had a huge grin on my face.
Maybe today wasn't so bad after all.

Sienna Rose R (9)
Christ Church CE Primary School, Lichfield

Egward The Egg

Dear Diary,

Today was horrible. *Crack!* That was my older sister. *Crack!* That was my younger sister. Oh no! It was my turn. A fat, greasy hand reached out at me and picked me up. The hand balanced me on a silver, metal bowl, before thumping me firmly against it. My shell was cracking and I could feel my yolk and my white oozing out into the bowl. Suddenly, a bit of my shell, with one of my eyes on, fell into the sugary, floury egg mixture. I saw two beady brown eyes stare into the mixture of sogginess and then a chubby hand fished around. Then I realised... the hand was looking for me!

Hi! Sorry about that long introduction. You probably didn't understand much. I'm Egward and yes, I am an egg. I mean, you probably think that being an egg is fun, easy, but no. Basically, you go from being born in a peaceful farm to being transported to a London house where you are most likely eaten. In my case, I'm being turned into a cake. Here's what else happened...

After five minutes of the hand attempting to find me, I was eventually carried to a food mixer. The machine was switched on and a metal thing flung me around the bowl. It was not fun.

After that, the grimy hand scooped the mixture up and placed us into another tray. We were then put into a heated room. Really heated actually. A bit *too* heated...

Flo Grumett (11)
Christ Church CE Primary School, Lichfield

A Puppy

Dear Diary,

Today has been a strange day. I woke up with my partner, Buster. He is very kind to me. Even though he can get on my nerves, he is very nice to me. Unfortunately, my owner goes to work every day, he never stays home. Why do humans go to school or work? Whilst they were out, I roamed around the house, which is quite boring to do. Then, something miraculous happened. I was minding my own business, just wandering around until the sirens went. There was an ear-piercing noise. I heard a loud smash through the window and someone wearing a stripy top and a black hat came through the window. He rushed towards me with that awful, smug look on his face. The burglar (I think that is what he was) was a tall man with a pointy nose.

Before I could even growl, he had picked me up and put me in a bag. It was pitch-black inside. The breeze made the bag swing side to side. Helplessly, I lay down and rested.

Later that day, I was taken to a house. It looked very strange and haunted. He chucked me in and slammed the door. Looking around, I found the window to escape.

The next thing I knew, a girl had taken me to a place to be someone else's pet. A little girl came and picked me up. She had a beautiful smile. She took me home and I saw Buster. The girl was the daughter of my owner. I hugged Buster and he hugged me back!

Olivia Wickett (9)

Christ Church CE Primary School, Lichfield

The Angry Book Of The Dump!

Dear Diary,

Today, like any other day, I sat on the lowest possible shelf, hoping to be read. I had been bought thousands of years ago for Snatchton Hill Grammar School, which is very private. Since then, I have never been read. Strangely, today, I was in the middle of my daily nap when, out of the blue, a grubby, snaking hand grasped my spine and started tugging at me. I closed my eyes, hoping I was going to be read, but, instead, I was cradled around corners and into fresh air. I had never been outside before, so I was shivering like a baby yeti, perplexed.

Suddenly, I was flung high into the air. I landed in a smelly, filthy site. I decided I would take a nap to make things better but, when I woke up, I was still there!

Time passed and time came, time I used for sleeping and praying. Out of the corner of my eye, I saw a man looking very quizzical. All of a sudden, the peculiar man howled, "Come back, my beloved watch!" Still chanting for his watch, he saw me and charged at me. As he ran past, he picked me up and started to flick through my crisp pages.

I thought to myself, as he carried me off, *no wonder I tell the same story every time. I'm a book!* He took me to his house and I was so popular and cared for that I decided to settle down for a while.

Sasha Chambers (10)

Christ Church CE Primary School, Lichfield

Only A Dream

Dear Diary,

Today was the weirdest day! I woke up in the forest and I had no idea why I was there. As I started to get up, I turned into a butterfly. I started to fly.

On the journey, I met a shiny, beautiful unicorn. I felt curious about it, I was shaking. Suddenly, I went through a tunnel. I felt shocked. It led me to a jungle that had more butterflies. I met another butterfly, I was really excited. I liked her so much, we chatted all day and at teatime her mum made us nectar pie. After that, we played with her sister Phoebe. Phoebe was fun to play with. We only had half an hour to play with them.

After ten minutes, it was Emily the butterfly's tattoo time, which is basically a machine that stamps your wings so the pattern doesn't come off in a day. Then, it was time for her to play with me. We started to dig and found a crystal. We dug some more and it led us to Devon. We went to the beaches and tropical islands together. Then Emily decided to find a free hotel for butterflies where everything was free!

After a nice, delicious McDonald's we decided to get some decaf coffees. Emily only likes rainbow milkshakes, so I bought her one of those as well. I always wanted tea but in that world, you weren't allowed tea. Then, I woke up. It was just a dream!

Sienna P (7)
Christ Church CE Primary School, Lichfield

Paddington's Football Adventure!

Dear Diary,

It was the second half of Wolves vs Aston Villa, the score was nil-nil and my fellow teammates and I were determined to score and win.

"Yes!" the crowd screamed, 1-0 to Aston Villa, who were winning the match. Wolves were nervous to see if they could win. A minute later, we scored and then it was 1-1. It stayed 1-1 through extra time. In the nick of time, Aston Villa scored and all my hair stuck up.

(Next match)

Dear Diary,

We're back again but at our pitch, not at Aston Villa's pitch. After the first goal, we were winning 1-0. Dribbling confidently, Neves ran with the ball between his feet and shot but he missed. It was now the second half and we were still winning, "Come on boys, score!" The Aston Villa manager shouted. I thought they wouldn't score. Little did I know, that there were two minutes left, so they couldn't score but then they scored 1-1. Then I scored and won, then we won, "Yes!"

As it was a fabulous day, the manager built a statue of me and my scrumptious marmalade sandwich. He also built a statue of the sad, miserable Aston Villa players to celebrate our victory. That was the best day of my life, I became a champion!

Finley Pike (8)
Christ Church CE Primary School, Lichfield

A Day In The Life Of An Alien

Dear Diary,

Yesterday was probably the strangest day of my life. A few days ago, when I woke up, I found out that our planet, Zing, could be attacked by some terrible creatures, the humans, who have horrible strings growing out of their heads and only two eyes. They sounded like terrible beasts. However, I didn't know that I was going to bump into a whole group of them!

It all started when I was taking my new spaceship for a ride into space. Pulling the levers and pressing the buttons as hard as I could, I felt my body drop in my seat as the unreliable vehicle hurtled towards the ground as fast as you could say, "Oh no!"

After I had picked myself up off the ground, I saw, to my horror, a crowd of humans who were hurriedly trying to bundle me into some sort of object that they could use to capture me. I thought of my friends, who would never see me again, and I remembered how one of them had told me that if I was ever in danger, they would come and rescue me. That wasn't going to happen.

Before long, I reached a place where the terrible creatures took some of my slime and put it into a cylinder-shaped object. After the villains had put me back into the capturing object, I cried myself to sleep...

Erin Robinson (9)
Christ Church CE Primary School, Lichfield

The Incredible Diary Of... Ryan Giggs

Dear Diary,

Today was absolutely incredible! Arsenal was in an unbeatable form but at United, we were confident that we would triumph over our bitter rivals. As I got changed, I could hear the roars of 75,000 fans shouting and screaming before kick-off. Since I was just a little, shy boy in Cardiff, I'd been dreaming of fixtures this big and Man U vs Arsenal couldn't get any bigger! I was ready for the big time!

"Treat the game as normal as possible," Sir Alex reminded us as me and the players put on our sparkling clean boots. He said this in case any of us got too big for our boots. "We can do this!" I told Paul (Scholes) confidently.

We stepped onto the pitch. The atmosphere at the 'Theatre of Dreams' was electric. The referee blew the whistle loudly. David Beckham passed crisply to Paul who picked out a brilliant pass to Cantona. "Shoot!" yelled the fans and why not? He struck it perfectly, but *boom!* It smashed against the crossbar. Becks swung his foot back and hit it so accurately that it zoomed past the keeper's gloves and the net bulged.

Becks got us the lead, which changed the game! Bergkamp scored but who would be the hero...?

Louie Hollinsworth (9)

Christ Church CE Primary School, Lichfield

The Incredible Diary Of... A Champions League Football

Dear Diary

Today is the day I am going to be at my favourite player's foot. I am going to be kicked by him and volleyed into the air. This will be done by the one and only Cristiano Ronaldo.

I really wanted to be picked so while I was in the manager's office I wriggled my way to the top of the bag to make sure I would be picked. It was tiring. When he opened the bag he chose me, I couldn't believe it. I had been chosen to play the match in the Champions League Semi Final.

When the referee held me whilst the players were in the tunnel I felt nervous and anxious. The crowd were clapping and the players walked out. I was placed in the centre circle. Ronaldo was taking the kick. The whistle blew and it began.

I was kicked and volleyed around the pitch but a player then kicked me into the stand and I accidentally knocked a man's drink over. He was angry but I was just glad I didn't get wet. Then Bale kicked me so hard I went over the stadium and hit someone's car smashing the window. I was annoyed, I wanted to be back inside the stadium.

Another person kicked me in the car park and I hit another car.

I thought this would be my best day but it became a bad day.

Charlie Evans (8)
Christ Church CE Primary School, Lichfield

My Mother

Dear Diary,

The weirdest thing happened to my mother today! This morning, I got out of my comfortable bed like I normally would. I jumped down the stairs into the kitchen to have breakfast. When I got down the stairs, I said, "Good morning!" I had just started eating my chocolatey, yummy Coco Pops when the letters came, so I went to get them like I normally would, but something was different. There was a letter with a golden envelope. I rushed it to Mother. She opened it and it read, 'Tired of looking after your children? Well, go on holiday for only five pounds!' Mother was so happy she had to book it right away. She ran upstairs to text all her friends and call up a babysitter to look after us.

Dear Diary,

It was time for Mother to go on holiday. I was excited but my little brother, Theodore, was sad we wouldn't see Mother for two weeks. Mother was so excited that she jumped into the car and sped off in our little blue mini. Mother had packed the car and got on the tram.

An hour later, she had arrived at the hotel. Mother happily got into the sea and went underwater and swam around with the fish and the dolphins.

Martha Olive Grace Dean (8)
Christ Church CE Primary School, Lichfield

Ted-Ted And The Magic Bed!

Dear Diary,

I, Ted-Ted, am writing from Sophie's bed, as usual, about the interesting event that happened last night at midnight! First, Sophie read me a lovely story and then she gave me 108 kisses and then gave me a giant hug whereas Cottontail, the other teddy that Sophie rarely hugs, only got 100 kisses and she didn't get a hug whatsoever. The explanation for this is that Sophie likes me so much, much more. Anyway, back to the story. So I went down to the control panel and as I should have mentioned earlier, Sophie and I, sadly along with all the other teddies, live in a magic bed!

As I was saying, I went into the control panel and I flicked some of the strange switches and pressed the yellow, sparkly buttons. Suddenly, a deafening noise began to boom. "Five, five, five. Four, four, four. Three, three, three. Two, two, two. One, one, one, and we have lift off." There was a distant rumbling and I felt myself being lifted off the ground. We flew through space and landed in a sweet-scented land of Candyworld.

For around ten whole hours, we messed about jumping up and down. Oh no, the time! Will I be back for the morning?

Sophie Swallow (8)
Christ Church CE Primary School, Lichfield

The Diary Of A Football That Won The League

Dear Diary,

Today I was made which makes today my birthday! When I was put together and stitched I played a silly, mischievous prank on the person who created me. I rolled away and hid so they had to keep looking for me.

Dear Diary

I am constantly travelling around and I'm getting annoyed. No one wants to pick me and kick me around because they saw my colour was red. We got to one country today called England. I was made to feel welcome. I saw a sign so I knew I was in Manchester.

Dear Dairy

Today I arrived at the feet of a player. I was taken inside the stadium to play a game. Little did I know I was the football chosen for 94:20. This has been the best moment of my life. Let me tell you more... The game kicked off and it soon became 1-0 to Queens Park Rangers. Manchester City were not going to win the League. Another goal made it 1-1. The competition was still on. Another goal made it 2-1 and Joey Barton got sent off. Another goal made it 2-2. The pressure mounted.

In the ninety-fourth minute, Balotelli scored the winning goal! Manchester City won the League. The crowd cheered. I felt amazing!

Jack B (9)
Christ Church CE Primary School, Lichfield

Boots The Kitten

Dear Diary,

This might be an unusual diary. You might be reading this, yes, you Mr Smarty Pants, confused because I am a cat! This has been an extremely crazy day. Are you ready? Of course you are! So, here it is. My day started off doing my morning routine. I went through the air vent to visit my boyfriend, Thomas the cat. But, I ended up in a different world, entirely made out of cheese. I was in Cheese Land! But, oh no! I fell in a giant tub of cheese but I was not alone in there. I met Daisy, the racoon. She had been stuck in there for days! Luckily, we cheered up because we were saved by Super Raina. She was a chicken who also had a sidekick called Bow Wow the Great. We got out of the cheese tub, then we searched around Cheese Land and we found three large vents. I decided which one to go into. I chose the left one. I went in and in that one was... a dog! I ran out of that vent and closed it. I went into the next one and in there was... another dog! I ran out for the second time. This was it, the last one and, guess what? It was! I thought to myself for a bit on my bed. I thought, *I'm scared of air vents now.* So, that was my day!

Annie R (7)

Christ Church CE Primary School, Lichfield

The Incredible Diary Of... A Snail!

Dear Diary,

I am hungry. No one cares about snails. The gigantic, two-legged walking things could leave us a small piece. Not saying I'm jealous or anything but they can *walk* with real-life feet! On the subject of hunger, today I was starving! It was a hot, humid day in the middle of a big sunny bit and I was lying on my shell when it came floating out of the sky. It was flying, it was green, it was *lettuce!* It landed in the southern part of the garden. I ran to get it. Okay, I slithered really slowly.

Five hours later.

Dear Diary,

A dog! He ran up to me and grabbed me with his paw. I screamed and shouted but nobody heard me as he dropped me into his mouth!

I opened my eyes and I was dangling above the dog's mouth. *Crunch!* The dog's jaw broke my shell which was so big the dog couldn't swallow it. I came tumbling down. "Don't eat snails, Fuzzy!" I heard behind me, it was the dog's owner. I came face-to-face with a young girl, who picked me up and dropped me by the lettuce. Sadly, the slugs had eaten it. Oh no!

Sam W (9)

Christ Church CE Primary School, Lichfield

The Incredible Diary Of The Mermaids

Dear Diary,

You won't believe what happened today. It all started when I was on a calm beach and I thought something was very funny. I ran down to the deep blue sea and I started to swim. Suddenly, I saw a bright blue thing. I swam closer and closer, I was bubbling with excitement. Suddenly, I saw two more, now there were three. I got closer and I realised that they were mermaids. I said, "I won't hurt you, I promise."

"Okay, but what is your name?"

"Pearl."

"Do you want to come to the mermaid land?"

"Yes, yes." My mum and dad were on holiday so my grandma was looking after me. They turned me into a mermaid, I was so happy. I said, "I need to be back for 3 o'clock."

"Okay."

The mermaid land was really posh. I had some lunch and I had fish because we were in the water. I did not know what to do because I was so excited. I went to the juice bar, I had one orange juice and two grapes.

Soon it was home time. I was so sad when I said bye and they turned me back into a person.

Eve (9)
Christ Church CE Primary School, Lichfield

The Incredible Diary Of... Sugar The Great

Dear Diary,

I am just getting ready for my dance competition and I am so nervous! I hope I'll be alright. My sister Buttons and I are on our way. BoBo has her lyrical before me. BoBo is getting ready to go on now and I am going to go and watch her. She will be so good. It's Bobo's turn to perform, she's got this! I am so proud of her.

Now it's my turn to get my costume on. I'm really nervous. What if I fall or forget my dance or... or... I'll be fine, breathe, BoBo will support me. I think my best friend Mai is in the audience too, she will support me as well. It's my turn to perform, I'm doing a salsa dance. Here it goes...

Dear Diary,

I won out of thirty-two gerbils. Mai and BoBo hugged me and we had a party at Mai's house. We had seeds and pizzas and party poppers, it was so cool!

Dear Diary,

This is Mai and BoBo, Sugar fell asleep two hours ago. We kept on partying and having pizza and all of that stuff but we think it's time to go to bed!

P.S Sugar became Sugar 'The Great'.

Olivia D (9)

Christ Church CE Primary School, Lichfield

The Adventure Of Alvin The Hamster

Saturday 26th January

Dear Diary,

Today was an exciting day for me. The morning routine was normal but at 11:30am, a lady came and picked me out of the cage. I was pretty scared and wondered what was happening. I heard a lot of people talking and they put me in a small green box. It was pitch-black inside the box as I tried to nibble my way out. All of a sudden, the box was moving around, I felt freezing and everything seemed different. Then, I got placed on the floor, after a few minutes I felt warm again and was released from the dark box as brightness shone in my eyes. I noticed lots of exciting things, like a massive blue wheel, food, a cosy house and lots of tubes. I thought, *I might like it here!* I had some food and then went to sleep in one corner of the tube. After a busy day, I went back to sleep until midnight and then played on the wheel until 2am. Then I had a little sniff and went back to sleep. I kept on hearing friendly voices. I think they are looking after me.

I have enjoyed my big adventure and look forward to more fun tomorrow!

Harrison Mullins (9)

Christ Church CE Primary School, Lichfield

Cookie The Labrador

Dear Diary,

My name is Cookie. Today was my first day at my new owner's house. I woke up at around 6am just in time to hear my owner gently exclaim, "Be a good dog," and cautiously close the door. *Time to let the fun begin!* I thought excitedly.

I had only arrived at the huge house the day before and it already felt like home. Energetically, I leapt downstairs. When I had finally clambered down the stairs I smelt the delightful aroma of freshly washed socks. I was extremely excited when I found them under the sofa. The socks looked almost too good to eat but only almost. After I had nearly chewed them to bits, I decided to make some more mischief. Unbelievably, I couldn't find anything to do.

Miserably, I walked up the stairs towards my basket to have a nap. Halfway up the stairs, there was a bright green tennis ball! *How did that get here?* I wondered. After I had tired myself out, I clambered back up the stairs to bed. As I lay on my comfy, cosy bed I started to drift off to sleep. That was my adventure at my new home.

Emily P (8)
Christ Church CE Primary School, Lichfield

78

A Gerbil Called Buttons

Dear Diary,

It was morning again. Excitedly, I stretched my arms out, making my normal superhero pose whilst planning what mischief Sugar and I would get up to today. Suddenly, I heard loud footsteps heading towards our cage. It was Mama, just looking into her loving eyes made me feel guilty but there was no time to worry about that.

Finally, I heard the predictable words, "Be good gerbils, I will be back in a few hours!" That was it, the deafening sound of the door being slammed shut. We were alone... Racing up to the top of the cage Sugar and I pulled open the door and hopped out. Now the fun could begin...

As we had been in this house for a year now we knew every route and short cut to get to the magical, too-good-to-be-true fridge. Suddenly, the glorious fridge came into view. Sprinting as fast as we could, we opened the door to the amazing fridge. Jumping inside, I stuffed my mouth with the delicious cheese. It was scrumptious.

Both Sugar and I slept well after all of that food, we just have to hope Mama never finds out.

Beth D (9)
Christ Church CE Primary School, Lichfield

Fish

Dear Diary,

One day my owner Ben just woke up to the sound of his mum screaming at him to wake up. He did not want to get up but he had to if he wanted to go to Spain.

He finally got up and dressed. He picked me up and we went to the airport. Before we got on the plane we had to go through security. They asked Ben, "Is that a fish?"

"Yes," said his mum.

"We were going to bring him on holiday," said Ben. I then realised they had called another security person over to check if I could go. They said, "No." We walked off back home. Suddenly we heard a noise and it was the security shouting it was just a joke. "Of course your fish can go on holiday." I was swimming around like crazy. I was so happy.

The plane was ready and waiting for the passengers. I was in Ben's bag so no one could see me. Ben's dad fell asleep and he was snoring really loudly.

After a long time, my dad woke up and realised we were there. We got out and we were in Spain. We were very happy.

Ben Short (9)

Christ Church CE Primary School, Lichfield

The Incredible Diary Of... Matthew And Summerset Close

Hello, my name is Matthew and I go to a school called Everbridge High on Summerset Close in America. I'm a basketballer, my closest friends are called Mike, he's a footballer; Matt, he's a basketballer like me; Sofia, she's a cheerleader; Megan, she's also a cheerleader; and finally Luca, she's a netballer. All of these people play for our school and our mascot is Barry the Eagle. Yesterday was one of the worst days of my life because of the opponent team. We were against another school called Summerset Green High, and guess what? They cheated! We would have won fair and square, the only reason that they cheated was because we were winning and they were losing! So Barry, Megan, Sofia and the rest of the cheerleaders were cheering us on. Luca was waving from the crowd.

The score was 1-1, then I scored a hoop, so then it became 1-2, after that Summerset High got extremely angry and began to kick and push me and the team, and they thankfully got disqualified. I trudged home in the pouring rain to my house.

Emma H (9)

Christ Church CE Primary School, Lichfield

The Incredible Diary Of... The Football

Dear Diary,

Today was a nightmare because I got kicked around so much I almost popped. For the people it was fun but for me, it was tiring because I got kicked around so much. One of the players kicked me so high I went into space. I was going so fast that I cracked the moon in half. When I was falling to the ground, I was shouting, "Argh, help me!" Finally, I reached the football pitch and blasted through the ground. I went through the crust-mantle and the inner core, I went through so many other planets and finally, I landed, in the ocean! The sharks were swimming towards me and I said, "Uh oh."

Suddenly, there was a steam blaster, so I swam towards it before the sharks could get me. I went onto the steam blaster and it launched me up into the clouds. Suddenly, there was a giant aeroplane. It was flying towards me and it almost chopped me in half. The people in the aeroplane were very confused, they thought I was flying.

I fell to the bottom of the ground and I was at the football game again!

Is'rael Lorenzo Frazier (9)

Christ Church CE Primary School, Lichfield

Rebel Ruby

Dear Diary,

It was walk time, my favourite time where you get to run around and have fun. Anyway, I'm upset because Millie is going to uni which means I won't see her anymore.

"Come on Ruby."

"Woof."

It is sometimes annoying but when I hear 'bacon' that's when I wake up!

"Bye Ruby."

Success, I was straight in the kitchen scoffing the butter which is salty. Then my eye caught the prize, there it was standing in a basket... Millie's Christmas socks! I chewed, sucked and they were gone. I had to change into Rebel Ruby. I searched through the house. "Hmmm?" I remembered from dog Brownies, Ninja Nina. "Come out, come out wherever you are."

"You've found me, but you will never have my ninja skills," she said. "You'll never have my Christmas socks," Nina said.

"But they're mine," I whimpered.

"It's called revenge."
I was so sad, I was going to be told off.

Ava Saul (9)
Christ Church CE Primary School, Lichfield

Eagle And His Friends

Dear Diary,

I started as a baby bird, but what kind of bird? An eagle, one of the strongest birds. As I started to open my eyes, I realised I was being pulled to a giant, scary house by a box. The boy (who was my owner) was tickling me under the chin. "Hey! I'm not ticklish!" I screeched, but because I am an animal he couldn't hear me. "Hey!" I shouted. Okay, that was it. I managed to fly a bit and then started pecking the boy on the bottom.

"Ouch!" cried the boy. With all that fun we grew up together.

When I was old enough, I went on my own journey. First, I went to the beach and then I found a crab. I asked him if he wanted to play and he did.

After a while, we were good friends and went to a new place. It was town and there we found a pigeon. The crab and I asked him to be our friend very nicely and again, he said yes but the crab was run over by a car. We were sad but we had to keep going. Lastly, we got to the tiger's place and finally, our last friend.

Noah Lewitt (8)

Christ Church CE Primary School, Lichfield

Stanley's Super Day

Dear Diary,

Today I woke up all alone. My wonderful owners had left me in the middle of the night and now it was just me. I left the empty and quiet kitchen to go up into the highest floor. After that, I found a Superman's cape in the dressing-up box, Then I added another 'S' to make Super Stan. By the way, if you didn't know, I am a short-haired Lhasa apso. When I entered the large living room, I realised that the window was open, so I jumped out with a 1, 2, 3 leap. I was flying! I zoomed over to Bailey's house, who is my best doggy friend. Then I told him that my owners had disappeared.

"Mine too!" he said. "Let's go to Jump Extreme!"

So Baily and I made an invention that could carry two dogs in the air. It was kind of like a motorbike in the air, so we set off on our invention. When we got to Jump Extreme, we started playing happily on the trampolines. I jumped so high that I saw a play area, so Baily and I went to it and played. After that, we went home.

Bella Hoey (8)
Christ Church CE Primary School, Lichfield

Diary Of A Weird Kid

Dear Diary,

Today has been the scariest day... Okay, that was good but I can do better.

Today has been the scariest, most horrifying day in my life, ever. That was the best, okay, let's start... It all started when I went on a school trip with my owner. On that school trip, my owner wasn't just any owner, he's a weird kid but I'm just a normal dog. (Yes, I am a dog and I am writing this.) So it all started when we were on the coach. We got on the yellow, wonky coach. Everyone started to set up camp. Well, as you know, he's very weird so I bet you know what will happen. He set his tent up upside down but I turned it over. Afterwards, we went to bed and it was morning. I had just about resisted his snoring. We went to get food with the school. We went out with one of the teachers, Mr Chip, was showing us how to carve a chicken. My owner saw a monkey. I tried to stop him from chasing the monkey. After he chased the cheeky monkey back to camp, everyone had left. "Help!"

Sam Aston (9)

Christ Church CE Primary School, Lichfield

Che Adams

Dear Diary,

Today, I was in my comfy bed. I woke up and my manager called me, he said that the match was cancelled because someone robbed the stadium. Then, for the rest of the day, he was sad. Then at lunchtime, my manager called me again. He said there was another football stadium in Birmingham, so I got dressed in my football kit. I quickly got in my car and I drove to the football match. When I got there, I got out of my car and ran to the football ground. My match had started! I kept on running, then one of the players passed to me and I dribbled up the goal and I scored. The crowd went wild! Then after the centre kick, the other team kept on passing. They got closer and closer to the goal. Then they scored, then it was half-time. After half-time, they kept defending and we went to a penalty shootout. I went first for my team. Then I scored and the crowd went wild again. The other team went for a shot and my team saved it, so my team won and we all hugged each other, then we all went home!

Oliver Eades-Davies (8)
Christ Church CE Primary School, Lichfield

The Incredible Diary Of Raúl Jiménez

Dear Diary,

Today was a wonderful day because I scored a goal against Birmingham FC and Conor Coady scored one goal, but then Che Adams scored two goals so that made it two all. So then, I had to play in the semi-final.

Dear Diary,

It was a derby game. I was really scared. Yesterday we played Birmingham FC, today we play a new game. Jota took a kick-off and then I got it. I passed to Conor Cody. Conor Cody said, "Get into space!" I got into a space and shouted, "Pass!" He shouted the same and we did a pass. I ran up with the ball and I volleyed it in... goal! The crowd went wild. The goalie and the kids who were on the path ran up and jumped on me.

After the celebration, the other player booted the ball and scored so it was 1-1 and half-time.

Our manager Nuno told me to substitute for Vinagre and when it was the second half, Costa scored another but it hit the crossbar and went out.

The match then went to penalties and it was 4-3 to Wolves! Yes!

Joe D (7)
Christ Church CE Primary School, Lichfield

My Life As A Fairy

Dear Diary,

Today was crazy. I was having a walk in the forest and I bumped into a magic wand. I was so confused. Then I took a deep breath and touched the magic wand. Then, weirdly, I grew silky, delicate wings and got really long hair. I was really surprised and got more surprised when a door opened in a tree. I slowly entered the tree and I met another fairy who gave me a little yarn person. We finally went off to explore. First, we met a human. Well, not met, we found a human. When she saw us, she tried to slap us. Then, Yarny wrapped yarn around the human. After that, she raged so much she made a volcano. When the volcano erupted, a rainbow appeared. I spotted a door under the rainbow so I went in the door and I was back into a magical land. I saw a lovely house, when I went over to the house, I saw a unicorn! I slowly petted it, it neighed happily! I was happy! Then, I went over to my house. It was amazing! I saw the unicorn again, it neighed happily. It was a really good day, I loved it!

Emily Alderson (7)

Christ Church CE Primary School, Lichfield

The Diary Of The Odd Random Things (Like This)

Dear Diary,

Last night I had a dream, not any dream, but the oddest dream. It started like a zombie potato who slide down the banister onto a cat but trust me, it gets a lot weirder! Next, someone flushed the toilet and a tsunami of talking poos came out! (This didn't happen in real life, so don't expect that when you flush your toilet, that a tsunami of talking poos will come.) Then the zombie potato decided to steal DJ Dog's salad and put salt, vinegar, mustard, ketchup, mayo and a scoop of diarrhoea on it and I'm not going to say what happened next or should I? But then, DJ Dog got mad so he pulled out a massive sledgehammer and crushed the zombie potato but then a super, amazing, fabulous and exciting pig ran in and blew up the room because he was a super dumb pig. Probably dumber than me and I'm pretty dumb! Then a baby started flinging diapers in every direction. That's when my brain ran out of ideas but you're probably happy - that's the end of the mayhem!

Ethan Wileman (9)
Christ Church CE Primary School, Lichfield

The Incredible Diary Of... A Funky Football!

Dear Diary,

I have just experienced the worst day of my life. It started while I was waiting for the referee to take me onto the pitch. One of the fans threw a massive piece of plastic at my head when all the players came on. As the referee took me onto the pitch, in the corner of my eye I saw a fan with cake. My mouth started to water but sadly I was not able to get it. The game was about to start and I was placed in the centre. I was kicked around. I was going left, right, up and down. It was so bad. It started to rain and I wondered if it could get any worse - it did! Someone kicked my head into the post and then I went flying up the pitch and almost rolled into the goal but unfortunately, the goalkeeper dived and managed to save me. I was all muddy after that because his hands were covered in mud. There were players everywhere, I felt like a small insect. Now the players were picking me up. Eventually, at the last minute, someone got a penalty and guess what... they kicked me into space!

Oscar Mann (8)
Christ Church CE Primary School, Lichfield

Hattie The Cheeky Cat!

Dear Diary,

I just woke up on the top of the chair, ready to relax, when my owner came down. "Time for breakfast!" I ran into the kitchen and got my milk and biscuits. Then my owner left the house... Time for the fun to happen.

Running outside of the door I met my worst enemy, Mopsy. We started a fight for ten minutes and I lost! After that I was so worried that I sat by the fire with my sister. Then another disaster happened! I fell in the hot tub and got really wet and soggy! I couldn't get out and I accidentally scratched the head cushion.

I went into the garden and saw a mouse, now was the time to chase it! As I ran down the driveway the small grey mouse was nearly on the road. Then... *squidge!* The mouse was dead because a car came up the drive, my owner! Quickly, I ran back through the door into the living room and on the chair! It looked like I had been asleep all day. My owner came in and gave me a pat on the head. The amazing fantastic end!

Callie Rose Meakin (8)
Christ Church CE Primary School, Lichfield

May's Amazing But Scary Adventure!

Dear Diary,

Today has been the worst day ever! I was slowly waking up from my lovely nap when I was disturbed by this girl called Lucy. I was so exhausted from being trapped inside of a dark, dirty cage that I made up a plan. When she put me in my ball, I would jump out but because I was so tired, I almost fell asleep! Quickly, she scooped me up but I escaped and she didn't realise because I was so fast! Just at that moment, I saw a giant, hairy cat. It was creeping up on me like it was about to jump at me! So I ran for my life because I was so scared... I jumped at the first thing I saw. That's great, the beast couldn't fit under it and banged his head. I crept back inside my cage and hid. I was very excited because Sugar and Buttons were coming over for a playdate. We liked to play in our balls for ages. Then I went back to sleep by accident. I dreamt of a unicorn flying over a rainbow!

But that isn't it, Buttons woke me up so I put a blanket on her for some revenge!

Lucy A (8)

Christ Church CE Primary School, Lichfield

My Dog's Life

Dear Diary,

Today I woke up to Ebony. As I woke up she went to go and sit on the sofa and I went over. I always do this. Ebony always gives me fuss and strokes by my bottom which I absolutely love. I got a bit sad because she let go of me and went upstairs to get dressed. That's when I heard my Mum. I rushed to the bottom of the stairs to go and get my breakfast. It was the best. It is called Pedigree, it's a five-star recipe, the best ever.

After breakfast, I went for a lie down and just slept. That was until someone's huge feet climbed over me and started stomping up the stairs. They went out for a bit and I wanted to make some mess. I went upstairs and started licking socks. Yum! I also opened the fridge and ate all of the cheese.

They came back and they didn't look very happy with me so they put me in the back garden to make me think about what I had done. So now I am stuck outside. Well Diary, I will see you tomorrow. Bye. What will happen tomorrow? Hmm...

Ebony Luke-Bailey (9)
Christ Church CE Primary School, Lichfield

Pencil

Dear Diary,

It all started on a normal day, sitting on the top of someone's ear, in a real school that was very smart too. I was in a lesson and I suddenly got pushed hard down on the page. It was too unbelievable to believe it really. From the top of the ear, I was balanced on, I had an amazing view, or it was until that moment in time. I started to move and crawl around the school. It was very noisy. Slowly, I reached the fresh air at last. It was very noisy. I'd always wanted to get out in the fresh air for ages. As soon as I got outside I suddenly fell off the tip of their ear. Luckily, I climbed back up on the ear.

When we got back inside it was very hot and the teacher said, "Take that pencil off your ear and put it in the pot. As soon as I heard that I suddenly felt dark and cold. I was in the pot of doom. Whenever a pencil got put into the pot of doom they always thought that their owner would forget about them. It was the end of the day and my owner came.

Isla R (8)

Christ Church CE Primary School, Lichfield

Bow And Ruby

Dear Diary,

Today was the weirdest day. Let me rewind. So it started when I woke up and I heard a bang but I thought it was just from outside. So I went to brush my teeth, then I heard it again. I went outside to see what it was, it was a spaceship! It slowly came down and out came a bunny! I said, "Hello!"

He said, "Can you be my friend?"

I said, "Yes!" So we were friends. We went to explore my house and then we went out to the woods to meet the other animals. There were two cats, they were called Fatcat and Boots. We went to finish exploring my house and Boots found a key, a big, shiny key, but we couldn't find a door for it. Then, we heard a girl cry and we found the door! We opened it up, it was a candy world and we heard the girl cry again. We found her but she was happy. The sky was made out of blueberry laces and the sun was made out of a gummy bear, it was amazing! We played in the sweet candy world all day and it was fantastic!

Rosie May Wilkes (7)

Christ Church CE Primary School, Lichfield

Max And Meg

Dear Diary,

I am sick and tired of my sister and I being ridiculously used for no reason. Every day, we are used for herding sheep but the other day, while we were herding sheep, we got lost and found a really peculiar, strange building. It was an abandoned house! We both went inside and we heard a loud noise coming from upstairs. We both crept upstairs and suddenly, with a bolt of lightning, we completely vanished! We had gone back to the Stone Age! It didn't look the same. Suddenly, we ran into a forest through a field and had a break in a flowing stream. A wolf pack was coming to scout the area so we dashed into a tree stump but one of the wolves spotted us, so I attacked it to defend my two-year-old sister. We curled around and around, making a circle. I struck first but I purposefully missed but then he ran off because he'd stood on a thorn. I ran back into the tree stump but my sister wasn't there... But she scared me because she shouted, "Boo!"

Ethan Frost (9)
Christ Church CE Primary School, Lichfield

The Ugly Monkey

Dear Diary,

Today has been the funniest day of my ugly life. Life in Florida is amazing. You get bananas and also get free massages. Oh, by the way, my name is Wilson and I am a monkey that lives in Florida. So, let's carry on with the diary, shall we? My dad is the friendliest dad in Florida Monkey Forest. Yesterday, I decided to explore Florida to find bananas in the Monkey Forest. The thing was, all the monkeys in Monkey Forest ate them all. I was trying to find bananas in the banana store.

Whilst I was trying my hardest to find the banana store, an eagle swooped down to capture me and flew me far away from epic, amazing Florida. After about two hours, the eagle flew me over to Germany. I was one hundred metres in the air. I was petrified about how high up I was and I was wondering if the eagle was going to drop me. Then suddenly, the eagle flew me all the way back to epic, amazing Florida but then he said hello to me and I said hello back!

Wilson O (7)
Christ Church CE Primary School, Lichfield

Dr Who

Dear Diary,

Today was a frightening day. It all started when I got up. I thought I would go on a beautiful walk in the woods. Obviously, I brought my BFF, my sonic screwdriver. On the way, I got hungry, so I sat down and had a little snack. When I sat down, I dropped my sonic! I found out after my snack, I felt really sad. On the ground, I saw a little cat pawprint and a rabbit's one too. I saw them and thought to myself they could have stolen the sonic screwdriver! I got my motorbike and zoomed off to save it! I found the two friends and they were about to drop the screwdriver down a cliff! Quickly, I snatched the sonic screwdriver off them. Behind me, I heard Annie the cat saying, "We will try again!" to Rosie the rabbit. When I got home, I promised never to put sonic in my back pocket ever again and to share my delicious sandwich with it, not that it had a mouth. Then I saved the world again! I mean, who else would save the world without Dr Who?

Daisy Priddle (7)
Christ Church CE Primary School, Lichfield

Charlie Lakin

Today, I got up and went to football training with Che Adams and Lee Camp. Lee Camp went in goal and Che Adams scored three and I scored five. Then, we went to the match with the rest of the Blues. We played against Aston Villa at home. Villa started, Grealish passed to Tammy Abraham. Then Craig Gardner got the ball and passed it to Jacques Maghoma. He passed to me and I shot and scored. Villa kicked off to Grealish who shot and scored, one all. After half-time, Che Adams passed it to me, I passed back and he dribbled with the ball and got fouled in the penalty box. He shot and scored, the crowd went wild. Villa shot and missed, then Grealish got a penalty for diving and scored, the crowd booed.

Full time, Che Adams went first and shot top bins, then Grealish shot but missed because it went to wide. Then, Lee Camp took the next one and scored. Tammy Abraham missed and the Blues won! One of the Blues fans came out from Row 25 and hit Grealish in the face.

Charlie T (8)
Christ Church CE Primary School, Lichfield

The Incredible Diary Of...

Dear Diary,

I am exhausted. I was eating a piece of lettuce when Bob the snail came along. Bob said, "Why are you eating alone?"

I was quite annoyed that Bob was there.

"I'm taking this, thank you," said Bob as he took the leaf off of me and slowly slithered away.

"Come back here, you slow coach!" I shouted. Even that didn't make him happy and that is how we got into a fight on the trampoline. Because we are snails, we can't bounce very high so we roll instead. All of a sudden, Bob started to whack me with a stick so I picked a stick up and started whacking him. He poked me in the eye so I poked him in both of his eyes. He said, "Oww!"

Well, it wasn't long until he quit but I felt tired. Bob was eating a piece of lettuce and then I took a piece of lettuce and said, "Thank you."

Then, Kevin, the snail, came along and he's my second worst enemy. No, not again!

Charlie S (9)

Christ Church CE Primary School, Lichfield

A Crumbly Cookie!

Dear Diary,

The door smashed shut, a smile grew on my baked face as I pushed the top of the cookie jar and I jumped out, the kitchen floor was smoother than usual so I did a little tap dance to let the crumbles go crazy! The clank of cookie crumbles woke up the annoying fat cat who loves chocolate chips, I'm chocolate chips! My smile turned upside down as the feline creature leapt at the counter, smashing the pots. Without thinking, I flung my pot at the creature as it meowed in the distance. Oh I'll get you next time.

Suddenly, I felt something was not right, it was my gut. It was all wet and mouldy. I reminded myself of the crumbles. I dropped on the floor and I patted over the cold floor.

Finally, I rolled all over the crumbles and an idea popped into my head. I gracefully leapt onto the window sill and I taunted the numbskull cat. I felt so cold as the kitten crashed through the window and into the pond.

The door opened...

Simão de Sousa Revés (9)

Christ Church CE Primary School, Lichfield

A Dumb Fish!

Dear Diary,

The tank clattered into pieces as my owner whacked the door open. He looked confused at the sharp glass on the clean floor. As he rummaged out of the room I had a plan. This distracted me a lot because he kept on farting. He took me out to the most boring shop ever. So, I kind of jumped through the open window to a dark, gloomy drain. This was worse, I could smell dog dung. I could not stand the smell, it was worse than horse and cow dung.

Freedom! I was in London. I could see buildings towering over my fish head! Big Ben was in my face because I was in the River Thames. The Shard was poking at my face like it was falling on my head.

Within seconds, I leapt up to the top of the London Eye, I was really high. It was a really nice view. I could see everything, but then I fell...

At the speed of light, I was dashing down to the rock-hard floor. Then I teleported back home before my owner opened the door. I now had wings...

William Crawford (8)
Christ Church CE Primary School, Lichfield

I'm Lost In The Falls

Dear Diary,

Today, I was strolling through the park when I saw a pile of leaves. I decided to take five giant steps back and count to three. One, two, three. I ran up and about a metre away, I jumped. It looked like a type of maze, but with leaves. I hate mazes. I tried to jump up to get out, but it was no use. I couldn't reach the exit. I had to follow the path. When I turned a couple of corners, I saw a spiky ball. It pricked me and said, "Oh, get out of my way, you penguin!" Then, I felt sad because whenever I got hurt, my mummy would give it a magic rub and kiss it better, but she wasn't there so she couldn't help. Then, out of the mist came a big badger who stood up for me and showed real care. She asked me what was wrong and I confessed, "I want to go home!" So, kindly, the loving badger showed me the way out of here. But, now, here I am worrying about what will happen to Mrs Badger and the spiky hedgehog.

Euan Barnby (10)

Christ Church CE Primary School, Lichfield

The Plate Plot

Dear Diary,

Today, I hoped for some sort of luck so that I didn't get food smothered onto my face, yet, today was very much the same.

I didn't get any surprises until lunch when the family that I serve food for had a roast dinner. I got placed onto the table and badly decorated with potatoes, gravy, Yorkshire puddings, broccoli, carrots and string beans.

After most of the food was demolished, it was time for a rinse. As you probably know, you can't just rinse a plate, you need to put it in the deadly wave (the dishwasher). I'm completely petrified of the life-taking whirlpool but it would be done sooner or later.

I sat impatiently in a space inside the monster when I saw the gushing water. In the space of a second, all the clear water winded me as it hit my china hard. Two uncomfortable hours later, I was carefully put back into my home (the cupboard) and got to rest until the next horror-filled day.

Sasha Beddoe (9)

Christ Church CE Primary School, Lichfield

The Incredible Diary Of A Footballer

Dear Diary,

I had a brilliant day. I drove to Old Trafford, I was playing football. We played horrible Wolves. We were one-nil up but Wolves scored. With five seconds to go, we scored. After that, we went to Molineux Stadium, we played Liverpool. We were one-nil down, but I booted it up the pitch. We scored five minutes to, we won and it was all because of me. Then, we went to another stadium and we played Brazil. We travelled a lot more and we won a lot more. After that, we got in Interwood FC. Then, everything went wrong. We lost a lot of games, we couldn't get it together. The team supporters weren't happy, so we got out there and showed them what we were made of, so we played a match and scored ten and the other team scored ten so it was a draw. We went through to a penalty shootout, they started. It was Joe, the goalie, he saved it. Then it was our team, I scored and we won! I was so happy! I am awesome!

Daniel Somerfield (8)
Christ Church CE Primary School, Lichfield

The Incredible Diary Of...

Dear Diary,

Last night, a terrible accident occurred. *Boom! Bang! Crash!* I tumbled out of bed. I stood up and looked through the pitch-black. I saw a light, it was coming from another teddy. I walked over to him. He was prepared to help me, but only if I gave a message to his friend. So, while everybody was asleep, we set off on a journey to get back to the top of the bunk bed. Once we were at the base of the bunk bed, the teddy said, "Farewell, don't forget my message!"

"Okay!" I said. So, I wrote it on my hand, then I began to climb. By the time I had gotten halfway up, my knees were aching like I had just run a marathon. Each step I took caused me more and more pain. By the time I reached the top of the bunk bed, I fell asleep. This morning, I told everyone about my amazing adventure last night and, thanks to my hand, I didn't forget to deliver the message.

Kay Mellor (9)

Christ Church CE Primary School, Lichfield

Jennifer Hudson

Dear Diary,

Today was the weirdest day of my life. It all started when I had eaten my breakfast and I was on my way to The Voice studios. I was very excited because it was the battles. As soon as I got there, I could see a crowd of miserable people standing outside the building. I wanted to see what was happening so I went to the front of the crowd where all the judges were. I asked Tom Jones what was happening and he said that someone was in the building and had locked the doors from the inside. Next, we saw them spinning around on all of The Voice chairs. He was dressed in black from head to toe and the black hoodie he had on said 'Watch Out For Me!' Then I had an idea. We got a rope and we climbed up and then went down into the building. We brought another rope and when he wasn't looking, we took him by the hood and he went to the police. Then, we partied all night long!

Lauren W (7)
Christ Church CE Primary School, Lichfield

Ronaldo

Dear Diary,

This day was the weirdest day ever! I was so tired, I didn't want to go to the match, but I had to. I was so tired, I went the wrong way and ended up in the sewer. After, they wondered where I was, but the game was going to start in ten minutes. I was playing the ninja turtles. I was happy because I won!

When I got to Wembley Stadium, I couldn't get in, but I had got the keys. I played after that and I scored a brilliant goal and it was half-time. Me and my team got a McDonald's. I had a big chicken wrap and a chocolate milkshake. It was so yummy and delicious. I wanted another one.

After, it went on, but they didn't see me. I got sucked up by a vacuum cleaner! It was so full, it spat everything out! So I hurried back to the match but I felt sad because they had scored without me! There were penalties and we won the European Cup! Hooray!

Sam Smith (8)
Christ Church CE Primary School, Lichfield

Barney: A Day On The Beach

22nd August,

Dear Diary,

Today it is August 22nd and it is the summer holidays. I was excited because I was going to the beach in Aberdyfi, Wales. When we got there, I ran into the sea and got my other ball. The curls on my back stood up and my eyes stung whilst looking at a crooked jellyfish which was right in front of me. Macy and Mikey dragged me to the crabbing decking. When they caught a crab, they smelt fishy and salty. I wanted to eat one, but Macy and Mikey put them in a bucket! But the bucket fell and I grabbed the biggest one and ran off with it! I put it on the jellyfish. Oww! I howled and it escaped into the sea very quickly. I looked for it but I could not find it in the sea. But, my favourite bit was the sand dunes because the long grass whooshed in my fur and Macy and Mikey were chasing me. You can see for miles on top of the sand dunes! I love my life!

Macy Elizabeth Morgan-Ford (9)

Christ Church CE Primary School, Lichfield

A Normal Casual Day In The FA Cup

Morning

Dear Diary,
At 11am, I got to the amazing, fabulous venue. I rushed straight to the clean, fresh changing rooms and me and Nyland got changed. When we were changed, our manager had only just arrived. About twenty-nine minutes later, the rest of the players arrived. We told them they were late but they said they weren't because kick-off was at 12pm.

Afternoon

Dear Diary,
We were against Wolves and they got kick-off but as soon as they played the ball, I stole it. I ran straight towards the goal, it took me five minutes. Coady kicked Kodjia in the privates, so I got a penalty and I scored off Patrício and it went in. Then Neves scored in the seventieth minute. When Jiménez shot, Nyland saved it and booted it up into the goal. At the eighty-ninth minute, Jiménez shot, so we drew.

Oliver Purkis (8)

Christ Church CE Primary School, Lichfield

Rosie The Jewel Thief

Dear Diary,

Today was a nightmare. I only managed to capture a million jewels and every day I clutch ninety-nine million jewels, huge difference! As normal, the police came after me and as normal, I escaped to the mines that led to my jewel-covered cave of secrets. Suddenly, a spine-chilling lightning bolt hit me and *poof!* I was in Buckingham Palace!

"What is this? Are you going to poison me or something?" I yelled.

"No," stated the polite queen, "we simply just invited you to tea, Rosie, and want to allow you to have two weeks living here. After that, we'll see what your attitude is to thieving."

After a week, I was enjoying some British meals and drinks, like Her Majesty, Queen Elizabeth the second of England. I also dressed like her. For a bonus, she crowned me her long-lost daughter, so I am her princess!

Lula T (9)
Christ Church CE Primary School, Lichfield

Enchanted

Dear Diary,

Today has been the weirdest day of my life! In the morning, I woke up to a lovely summery sun. Then I went out to the mirror and I found myself in a pretty, green, flowery dress. I thought about breakfast, so I went outside and all around were juicy pink mangoes. I went to pick a delightful mango but felt butterflies in my tummy. I had found a friend, "What's your name?" I asked. She said her name was Music and she came home with me. I felt excited and safe with Music. We had mango juice together. After that, her eyes turned black. She had been cursed by a nasty, bad wizard. Quickly, I raced out the sweet little orange cottage. I felt frightened of her! Next, I found a wand on the spring grass. I saw pinks and blues on the wand. Then, I started running back to Music. After I blasted the wand at Music, she changed personalities!

Corinna S (7)
Christ Church CE Primary School, Lichfield

The Diary Of My Squashed Shoe

Dear Diary,

It's me again, the shoe. I have been getting bruises all over, from top to bottom. I am so tired of being trampled on and squashed. I need someone to look after me because these feet are getting way too smelly, stinky and big.

Dear Diary,

I woke up happy as we were going on a holiday! I wondered where we were going. It was horrible, it was a shop. I was placed on a small shelf and then put in a pitch-black cupboard. Doesn't anyone care about a small shoe like me? Get me out of this horrible cupboard! Seriously!

Dear Diary,

When I got taken out of the small cupboard I found myself in Africa, seriously? I am very hot here! The good news is though that I found my other pair, the other shoe I have been searching for. This isn't such a bad place after all. No smelly feet and my BFF with me.

Orla G (8)

Christ Church CE Primary School, Lichfield

Coco And Belle

Dear Diary,

Today was the craziest night of my life. I'll tell you what happened all the way from when I went to bed. So my owners tucked me and my sister, Belle, in and shut their old, broken bedroom door behind them, closing it with a big loud bang! As soon as that happened the big white back door creaked open - *creeeaakk!* Out from the pitch-black night came two men dressed in black with purple, scary masks. Belle was scared to death, me on the other hand, I was loving it. While I was loving it Belle was hiding under her snuggly light blue blanket. She didn't even realise what was happening here.

The next thing I knew was that I was in a dusty old car. "I think we're on a hill?" I told Belle.

"Yes we are!" boomed a mysterious person hiding in the shadows...

What will happen to us...?

Phoebe Newman (9)
Christ Church CE Primary School, Lichfield

Mrs Pilmore, Our Head Teacher

Dear Diary,

I woke up and had my breakfast and I put on my smart clothes and then I got in my red car and got out of my red car and went into my office. Then my white telephone rang. I quickly picked up the telephone and said, "Hello!" The man told me the delivery would be here tomorrow. I didn't know that it would be here tomorrow. Then I carried on with my letter. I went to the printer. I was worried, I hoped the printer would work. Then I pressed the print button, suddenly, the letters came flying out of the printer. I was covered in letters! I said, "Help me! Help me!" Mrs Davenport opened the door and then all of the letters went flying over everybody in the school. Then I had a super idea and I turned the printer off! I tidied up all of the letters and everybody was safe. I was so happy!
Mrs Pilmore

Lydia Withers (7)
Christ Church CE Primary School, Lichfield

The Incredible Diary Of Zip The Snake

Dear Diary,

Today, I woke up and I had no energy. Suddenly, a warm flash of sun beamed down on me and that gave me the energy to hunt. I stretched and yawned and slithered down the tree.

Finally, I was down the tree and I reached the ground. Suddenly, I heard a rustle through the grass and a yummy, tiny hairball with a worm sticking out the back of it popped out. I went after it. I looked left and I looked right, but the mouse was nowhere to be seen. I flicked my tongue out but nothing could help me find it now. I went deeper into the jungle and I had been looking for hours.

It was getting dark, so I had to get back to my tree. Then, I heard a high-pitched squeak come from my tree. It was a delicious delivery right to my tree stump of a mouse. I went to sleep with a full belly, dreaming of my next adventure.

Ethan Tonks (9)

Christ Church CE Primary School, Lichfield

A Secret Llama

Dear Diary,
Today was another boring Monday in Llamasville, or so I thought. I work at the llama police force and I was driving my beautiful Aston Martin Vanquish. Suddenly, while driving, my phone rang. At first I thought it was my boss calling because I was late but it was the body of elders, how surprising. On the phone they said I was going to be a detective in MI6 but that was in London. Kindly they let me into a hotel that was called Blue Monkey Casino.
When I got to the place I had a look around the place. Soon my watch was vibrating. I thought if I tapped it, it would come up with a screen and it did. It said the top five criminals were here. Just as I got set it said: 'Mission accomplished', somebody else must have completed the mission. I don't think I will ever know who he actually was...

Bentley Felton (9)
Christ Church CE Primary School, Lichfield

The Amazing Diary Of A Pencil

Dear Diary,

Today was the ultimate day of my death. It started out fine with a nice, lovely picnic with a summery breeze. I was with my loving girlfriend called Jessie. We were writing stories on the picnic blanket and also, we brought a sharpener to sharpen ourselves. Oh yeah, I nearly forgot, my name is Joe. I should probably explain.

It was a sunny morning yesterday and I went to play pencil football. I was playing against Villa, and guess what? It was 4-2. Yes. So that's the start of the explanation. Wait, just need to sharpen myself...

Now I've finished sharpening, wait, what was that sound?

Oh no, with a crack, I've just snapped in half! Now I'm writing this from pencil heaven, don't find it weird! You can write all you want and not die! From Joe the pencil.

Ava C (8)

Christ Church CE Primary School, Lichfield

The Incredible Diary Of...

Dear Diary,

Today was a wonderful day because I was in the final against the boring Wolves. It was marvellous as I walked on the pitch. The crowd went wild as my football club, Birmingham City, walked on the pitch and I, the captain, got the amazing, special football. The person behind me, Jota, kicked me and almost made my shoe come off. I said, "Jota, why did you do that?"

He said, "I wasn't looking where I was going!"

When I started the match, I passed to Jota. He carried the ball forward and passed it to me, then a defender from Wolves kicked me in the shin. Then, it was a free kick for us. The ball hit the crossbar. Then, it went to the second half and Jota scored. The fans went wild, then I scored a penalty! Ten seconds later, the full-time whistle sounded. We won!

Ben Hollis (8)
Christ Church CE Primary School, Lichfield

The Dog Invasion

Dear Diary,

One hot sunny day last month, I was fast asleep and I heard a sudden creak. It was the front door! As soon as I woke up and triple-checked the house and found that nobody was in, I decided to cause some mischief. Just then, the door creaked again, but this time, it was my mom and dad coming in with a little dog that I had never seen before. Her name was Ada. I was, of course, jealous! So, I tried to get rid of her. First, I took her to Egypt and, as I got on the aeroplane, she jumped into my bag. When I got home, she popped out of my bag. I tried to leave her in Africa, but she hid in my cap and came home with me. My last idea was to fly Ada to Jamaica and when we got there, I hopped back onto the aeroplane and Ada was in my back pocket! So, in the end, I just kept her.

Alina G (9)

Christ Church CE Primary School, Lichfield

Guinea Pig

Dear Diary,

Today I woke up, shaking some yellow hay off my back. Suddenly my sister rose and started to run around. Next, we got some lovely hay and water. Out of nowhere, we heard the dreaded black cat that always tries to eat us. So we hid and the horrible thing went away. Next, we got to our second plan of the day. We kicked the front of the hutch down. It was the final of the Caribo Cup between Man City and Chelsea. We really wanted to go. We escaped out the broken door and under the gate. We got on a bus to the game.

After three hours we got there. We watched all the game and it went to penalties and Man City won! Now Man City has won the Caribo Cup again, they have won it multiple times before. We were thrilled.

By the time we got back, our owners were home.

David Cartwright (9)
Christ Church CE Primary School, Lichfield

The Life Of A Race Car

Dear Diary,

I was in bed asleep and I dreamt about cars, I love cars, especially race cars. They are my favourite car. When I woke up I wanted to drive one. That was the day of my birthday and guess what? I got a race car! Today I am going to race for the first time. I hope I win and I will tell you all about it when I get back.

Dear Diary,

I won against 20 people. I really shouted. My car was very dirty so I sprinkled it with water. It was soon ready to race again. I then got to build a cabinet for my trophy. Next I went to Tesco to buy milk, butter and egg and sugar to bake a cake for my gran. I am now going to my gran's soon but first I have to buy lunch. I will get a baguette with ham and a drink. I also need to plan out my next race. Bye Diary.

Thomas Robertson (8)
Christ Church CE Primary School, Lichfield

The Day I Was My Dog

Dear Diary,

Today changed my life. Today, I woke up from an amazing dream, but something didn't feel right. Strangely, I felt very weird, which probably wasn't a good sign. I felt very hairy but too hairy. As soon as I awkwardly jumped out of my bed, I tried to stand up on my two feet, but I didn't have the strength to. I had noticed that I had a curly, short tail. I thought to myself for a second, *am I a dog?* I thought to myself again, panicking, *how did this happen? When did this happen?* I kept thinking and thinking to myself how this tragic mess could have happened in the first place. How would I ever go back to normal when I was in my dog's body? What if it was permanent and I had to live like this for the rest of my life?

Mia Lewis (10)
Christ Church CE Primary School, Lichfield

The Lost World

Dear Diary,

Today it has been the most exhausting day ever. It all started when I woke up in my comfy bed. I was walking then a sparkle caught my attention. The blossom tree looked unusual. It never had pink sparkles around the blossom tree. So I decided to touch the blossom tree. Suddenly, I teleported to the lost world! "Help me, please, someone," I shouted. Suddenly, I heard a footstep behind me. "Hello, is there anyone behind me?" The footsteps got closer and closer. I wondered who was the person behind me? My heart was racing, I could hear my heart racing going *dump, dump*. The shadow got closer and closer. I was too scared to open my eyes but I knew I had to keep my eyes open. Then suddenly I realised I was in an old-looking museum...

Nancy Florence Whiteman (8)

Christ Church CE Primary School, Lichfield

The Incredible Diary Of The Annoyed, Unhappy Pencil!

Dear Diary,

Today has been the ultimate disaster. I'll start from the boring morning. I was next to my darling, lovely girlfriend (who will soon be my loving wife). We were in our relaxing pencil pot which we love, then a couple of hours later, the pupils arrived. Luckily, we didn't have to be used at reading because you don't really need a pencil at reading. Twenty minutes later it was maths, but we luckily didn't get used. Then, a couple of minutes later, I was being sharpened which really hurt! Then a little kid came along and I really mean little. He started to bend me. "Ow!" I screamed. Suddenly I could hear a big crack and I knew I was about to die...

So that was the day. I died. It's much nicer up here in pencil heaven.

Oliver C (8)

Christ Church CE Primary School, Lichfield

Dog Days

Dear Diary,

Today I woke up very tired, then I went to see if any of my owners were awake. Two of them were, two of them weren't. One of my owners came down and gave me some breakfast and a morning walk.

A couple of hours later, after my walk, two of my owners went to school. I went to work with my daddy owner. While I was there I ran and messed up his paperwork. Everyone loves me. Then I ripped up a paperwork presentation about dog food, because it was dog food. Who doesn't like dog food? Then my daddy got mad at me because he needed it for a meeting, but then his meeting came and I saved the day by being his model. I sat there very proud of myself.

Then I finally came home. It was the best day ever. From Teddy the dog.

Harriet Darcey Alford (8)

Christ Church CE Primary School, Lichfield

The Terrifying T-Rex

Dear Diary,

The other day, I was casually ambling up a volcano in search of food. As I got near halfway, I heard a distant rumble and thought nothing of it. I continued to ascend, wondering what I would find at the top. As I approached the top I heard an ear-piercing crash. A stampede of rhinos appeared in my stomach and I realised the volcano I was standing on was about to erupt! I turned and fled at the speed of sound. I kept running into rocks and trees but, nevertheless, I carried on going. Desperate to escape, I saw my chance, a ledge to jump onto that was higher than the lava. Patiently, I waited for what seemed like days, nervously watching the lava pass by. A few hours later, the lava had come to a halt and I sprinted to my family.

Rhys Davies (10)
Christ Church CE Primary School, Lichfield

A Day In The Life Of Mo Salah

Dear Diary,

Today, I did lots of different things. First, I did loads of sleeping so I could have loads of energy in the match. Then, I ate my usual nutritious, healthy breakfast before I prayed for luck for the match. After that, I went back to sleep to get even more energy to use in the match. When I woke up again, I decided to play with my son to keep my interest. Afterwards, I had my lunch with all of my teammates before getting onto the bus to Anfield. Then we got changed into our training kits and got onto the pitch. We then got changed into our match kit and discussed the tactics. As I walked out onto the pitch, it felt amazing as usual. At the end of the match, we won two-nil and we went to the top of the league.

James Hargrave (10)

Christ Church CE Primary School, Lichfield

How To Train Your Dragon

Dear Diary,

I was walking in a village and I heard a horn noise. People were running and screaming and a black dragon got me by the shoulder. After that, I woke up and I was terrified because there was a whole world of dragons and I hid behind a rock. I was breathing very fast! Then the black dragon was in front of me. It was nice, but I thought I was out of my mind! But I wasn't. After a while, I went back to the village to make a saddle. Then, we went back and I put it on the dragon and I was holding on very tight on its tail. It flipped its tail and I went flying onto its back. Then it landed and I was really still. Then I went back to the village and told my friends but they didn't believe me, but I knew it was real!

Alfie Edward Smith (8)
Christ Church CE Primary School, Lichfield

The Incredible Diary Of... Me, Phoebe The Cat

Dear Diary,

Let me tell you all about my summer holiday! So it all started early on the first Saturday of the term. It was 7am and everybody was awake, so I decided to start meowing to get my breakfast. Lily gave it to me and my brother Rufus, instead of her dad, Rob. Thanks, Lils! It was so delicious! Later that day, Lily picked me up and held me like a baby! I mean, I am not a baby! When she put me down, I went outside to chase birds! Yum, yum! (By the way, if you are reading this and you aren't me, you probably don't like birds...) Anyway, back to the story! It was time for my tea, so I went back through the dirty, hairy cat flap. My food was already there! I'm not quite sure who did it but at least I had it!

Lily H (9)
Christ Church CE Primary School, Lichfield

Mischievous Ernie And Bertie

Dear Diary,

Bertie and I have just had the best adventure ever! Our story starts at home in Thorpe Close, number 16. Our dad, Lloyd, said, "Behave well guys, or else..."

After he left the house, we had our plan all ready, so we made our escape. We got out our Cat-O-Mobile and drove to Alton Towers! Now the fun was about to begin!

We first went on Octonauts, then Runaway Mine Train. We enjoyed Wicker Man. Bertie screamed on Oblivion but I loved it. I loved Smiler but Bertie was not too sure.

After five hours it was time to go. We got in our Cat-O-Mobile and drove home. I climbed in by the window and Bertie by the garage. We had the best adventure of our whole cat lives!

Lloyd O (9)
Christ Church CE Primary School, Lichfield

Katy Perry

Dear Diary,

Today has been the best day of my life! I woke up and I opened my lucky, enchanted cereal box. Suddenly, two lucky microphones popped out of the box. Slowly, I picked up the lucky microphones and headed out to practise with George Ezra. I went backstage and sung into the lucky microphone so I could test out what it did. "George!" I shouted. "Try out this lucky microphone!" He dashed to me but he was shouting something to me,

"Check out what I found!" he exclaimed.

It was a shimmery, gleaming gold microphone. They said it was showtime so me and George rushed onto the stage and sang 'Roar'. Suddenly, we both turned into famous pop stars...

Charlotte Abbishaw (8)
Christ Church CE Primary School, Lichfield

136

Two Gorillas

Dear Diary,

Today I had a fun day. Charlie and I were causing some mischief. We threw things at people climbing on our high ropes and were having a good laugh. I climbed on a net and picked up a banana and threw it at someone. It was a direct hit.

Charlie had a great idea. "Let's escape."

I replied, "How?"

He said, "Smash the glass."

We climbed up and started to bang on the glass. After a while, we broke through.

"Time for some fun," I said to Charlie.

Charlie said, "Where do we go first?"

"The gift shop. Charlie, check out this toy gorilla, he looks like you."

"Yes, it does."

William Lester-Jones (8)
Christ Church CE Primary School, Lichfield

The Incredible Diary Of...

Dear Diary,

Today, I was rudely disturbed whilst I was having my afternoon nap. A woman picked me up carelessly and put me in her bag. I was pretty sure she was stealing me from the sports shop. By the way, in case you were wondering what I am, I am a football. After a long time, that felt like a whole year, I finally came out of the dusty, rotten bag. I was in some sort of box. Slowly, it grew darker and darker until I was sealed in. After a day or two of travelling on a ship, I came out of the tight, sealed box. Unfortunately, as soon as I came out of the box, I was wrapped in blue and orange wrapping paper. I could hear a young boy laughing and celebrating as he unwrapped me.

Robbie Allen (10)
Christ Church CE Primary School, Lichfield

Johnny English

Dear Diary,

Today, I went on another mission. They gave me a hard one to do because I am a spy. I went on a mission and I went so far that I went on an aeroplane. When I got there, I saw the guy straight away. I ran and ran to him but he jumped to the other road, so I went on a train to get to the other road. Then he climbed down a building so I went after him. Then he got to the bottom and I got what I needed and I went back on the aeroplane. I asked some people to put my case away with one of the keys in it. When I opened my case there was nothing in there. I was looking around, but I did not see the key anywhere, so I had to get another key, so I went to get another key!

Harry Trivett (7)
Christ Church CE Primary School, Lichfield

The Explorer

Dear Diary,

Today I found an extraordinary discovery. First I didn't know what it was but then I did. It was a hidden temple. I peeked inside and found tonnes of valuables. I explored more and more but just found more traps. Suddenly, I found what I was looking for, the Golden Cutlass. Suddenly, the temple was closing. I ran incredibly fast and I just got out. I could hear bangs, pows and zaps and then the temple was demolished.

I explored more of the jungle and found a good place to set camp but didn't want to stop. I travelled 1,000 miles through the jungle and missed my family but I made myself a cup of tea and carried on.

Leo Cooke (8)

Christ Church CE Primary School, Lichfield

The Amazing Alex

Dear Diary,

Today was a great day! To start with, I woke up in the morning and I was in a carnival. I found an exciting village and in a village house, there was a diamond axe and a diamond sword. I went through a forest and I found a mine. I found a diamond one. Unusually, I screamed. It was a great scream. A horse ran up to me and she was wearing armour. I made her a name tag and I called her Mia. I hopped on Mia and went home. I had some food and went back out to the forest. I cut down some trees and I felt so lonely, so I found some friends. I found them and they came and helped me and lived with me. I went out with my friends and I felt very joyful!

Phoebe Lucy Tole (7)
Christ Church CE Primary School, Lichfield

The Discovered Unicorn

I live on a boring farm. Today my mum said it was time to get rid of my horse. I didn't want to but she wanted to sell it. I looked in my book and then I figured out that my horse was actually a unicorn. I quickly ran out and told my mum, but before I could even tell her I saw that my horse was right behind her. I was shocked and surprised. I secretly grabbed my book and I read it out to my horse. I stroked her mane and I said, "You will grant my wish and you will become a unicorn." I was so shocked and fainted when it happened. I would never be lonely again. I ran off to tell all my friends but they have to keep it a secret.
Bye Diary!

Georgina H (8)
Christ Church CE Primary School, Lichfield

My Dog

Dear Diary,

One day, I woke up with a smile. It was Saturday! I wondered what mischief I could get up to? Thankfully, Mum said she was going to the shops. I ran downstairs and I opened the fridge and I grabbed the bacon and cheese. Next, I remembered there were a lot of flowers outside. I hurried outside and ate the lovely flowers. When I had finished eating I ran inside and wrapped a toilet roll all around the house until Tabby, next-door's cat, was staring at me. Next time I will get her back!

Beep! Beep! Beep!

"Oh no, Mum must be here." I quickly ran downstairs and Mum gave me a big smack. I just fell asleep.

Oliver J (9)
Christ Church CE Primary School, Lichfield

The Dog Kidnapper!

Dear Diary,

Today was crazy but I will start from the beginning. I woke up and went to Mummy's room. She was fast asleep. I kept hearing footsteps behind me but no one was there. I looked behind me again, it was Mummy. I wagged my tail so much I weed. She said, "Why did you do that? Do you ever see me do that?" She went off to do something.

All of a sudden it went dark. It was like a bag around me. I was chucked into a big car. They then threw me into a cage. It was ginormous. There were fellow dogs in the cage but they didn't look very friendly. In the end, my mum saved me. Goodbye Diary, till next time.

Isabelle O'Grady (9)

Christ Church CE Primary School, Lichfield

Diary Of The Floating Diary!

Dear Diary,

Let me tell you about the strangest day of my life. Last night me and my sisters were having a snooze on the coach until something or someone began banging on the front door. Suddenly books began to fly in from nowhere, bursting through the room. We ran out shouting for help, hoping that someone would hear us. The door closed behind us, everything was still, everyone was still but something mysterious began to move. Me and my sisters tried to move back to open the door, it was slow motion. Sienna leaned onto the front door and suddenly everything began to move again. The mysterious thing was gone. It was like magic!

Zini V (8)

Christ Church CE Primary School, Lichfield

The Incredible Adventure

Dear Diary,

Today, I found a funny, annoying monkey and the monkey went, "Ooh ooh! Aah aah!" and led me to a temple. This funny, kind, annoying monkey led me to the yellow, bright temple and I found shiny gold coins. The monkey was little and beautiful. The monkey was nice and helpful and liked bananas. I liked him and he was weird and happy when he was in the temple. There was no one else and I kept finding more interesting things and lots of stuff and cute things. When the monkey came over to me, I was very happy. When I ran, the monkey found me again. Then, the nice, kind monkey came home with me.

Aiden Dixon (8)

Christ Church CE Primary School, Lichfield

Monkey Mischief

Today, it was a miracle. It was another rainy day at Oak Street and my mom went on another shopping trip to the shopping centre. The bad news was that I had to go but, suddenly, when we got there, it was invaded by monkeys! So, that meant it was the best day ever! I thought, *let's have some fun!* Then a monkey said, "We don't do fun!" and he swung away and started swinging everywhere. I didn't care. I went to every bed store in the whole of the shopping centre. Then, something horrible happened. One monkey bit a wire, but that was the wire of the whole city's power!

Kian Edwards (9)
Christ Church CE Primary School, Lichfield

Bob Bomber

Dear Diary,

Today was the worst day of my life. I had a shop of bombs and matches. Someone came in and bought one then ran into a helicopter and bombed my shop. I was so angry. I threw a bomb at his face which made him run for his life. I built another shop with grenades. Then I felt an earthquake, which made all my bombs shake and explode and my shop! So then I built a skyscraper. It was so high that it fell and got burnt. I made a cathedral which got smashed by a jumbo jet. Finally, I created a football stadium but, really annoyingly, it got burnt by a volcano!

Benjamin Roseblade (8)
Christ Church CE Primary School, Lichfield

My Day In Italy

Today, I visited the Leaning Tower of Pisa, it really looked like it was falling down! I decided to go up it. We took some photos of it then after we got down, we went to a restaurant. I had a margherita pizza and my mum had a lasagne with a glass of burgundy red wine. It was delicious. Tomorrow, we are going to Venice and we are going to go on a gondola down the canal and under the Rialto Bridge. It will be amazing! Did you know that there are no roads in Venice? You can only travel by boat. I'm really tired of walking, I'm going for a rest now. Bye-bye!

Phoebe Ann Jones (9)
Christ Church CE Primary School, Lichfield

Messi

Dear Diary,

Today, it was the best day! I went to football, but the dressing room exploded and it was made out of diamonds. I was very happy because we won 99-0 because we scored every minute and there were nine minutes of penalty time. This is how I scored 99 times. I tackled quickly to rapidly score and their goalie was slow and the ball went at 70 miles per hour and most of the time, I avoided everyone, that was basically half the time, plus I scored and I was the only one to score, so I got the World Cup!

Alex B (7)

Christ Church CE Primary School, Lichfield

The Overlord

Dear Diary,

Today, I went to school, but it was frozen so there was no school! We celebrated, but then we saw there was an Overlord. He had so much power, he could shoot lightning out of his eyes and he could shoot water and fire out of his hands. The Overlord had taken over the Earth, he was unbeatable and no one could stop him. He could fly and he had a repairing shield, it covered him and it was massive. Everything was his, he was rich and he had powers. He was unstoppable.

Will M (7)
Christ Church CE Primary School, Lichfield

Mario And The Grave Ghost

Dear Diary,

I was exhausted when I came back from my huge trip. First, I went to Kentucky, then France. After that, the USA, and then into the sky and to the past to see Black Bart, the outlaw. I did favours for a devil. A queen wanted her socks and her crown finding. I also met Michael Jackson!

Unfortunately, I had to pick up a sword and kill the devil and Black Bart to save people though.

Kind regards

Mario - king of video games.

Kane Ethan Williams (8)

Christ Church CE Primary School, Lichfield

Lionel Messi

Dear Diary,

Today I was so excited because it was the big match! The phone started to ring, it was my manager. I got into the car and I went to the stadium. When we scored, everyone was shouting. I was about to score. Someone slide-tackled me. It was a penalty. I was sweating so much! I thought I wasn't going to score but I did it!

Quickly, the ref shouted, "Last five minutes left...!"

Owen D (7)

Christ Church CE Primary School, Lichfield

The Day In The Life Of Frank

Dear Diary,
Today was the best day ever! I woke up and I said to my parents, "I'm hungry, give me crisps now!" After breakfast, I headed to McDonald's. When I got there, the queue was terribly long so I did what only thug dogs do, I went into the bin and found an old McFlurry cup. I also did my business in it and gave it to someone so that we could swap. That wasn't the best of it, I also robbed McDonald's!
#ThugDogLife
Frank

Thursday 16th,
Dear Diary,
Today I woke up in my McDonald's mansion with my six million chicken nuggets and two million cheeseburgers. As usual, I went downstairs and asked my maid for a cheeseburger and six chicken nuggets.
After breakfast, I went and got into my nugget Lamborghini and made people
feel poor.

Finally, I had chicken nuggets for dinner.
Frank

Friday 17th,
Dear Diary,
Last night I didn't get sleep at all. I woke up feeling sick in my nugget mansion. I decided to ring my maid from downstairs to bring me some nice warm nuggets to help get my cold out. After breakfast, I went to my computer and played Roblox for six hours and missed lunch! Finally, I put some Netflix on and called up my maid again to bring my dinner. At the end of the day, I got into bed and waited for the grubby day to be over.
Frank

Maddison Ford (10)
Hazel Slade Primary Academy, Hazel Slade

The Diary Of The Inventor

Dear Diary,

Today started off as a naff morning. There was no delicious bread for my toast, so I had to have cereal. Second, my car broke down, so I had to walk all the way to work. When I finally got to work, I needed something sugary to get myself hyped after such a morning, but there were no cupcakes or doughnuts left. *Why is today so rubbish?* is what I was constantly thinking. I still saw a bit of hope. As I am an inventor, I was thinking about what to invent when it suddenly hit me! I was about to make something that would solve all the problems I had had this morning. A cupcake-pooping, toast-making, awesome-flying, cuddly invention! It would be amazing! I would call it a unicorn! After all the celebrating, I realised that the hardest thing about being an inventor was actually making it; so, thinking really, really hard, I came up with a solution. I couldn't make this wonderful creature with lots of mechanics. I had to be like a witch or a wizard and put lots of things together in my potion. I figured out an amazing way to put all of the things in! An ounce of love and helpfulness, a cupcake, a piece of toast and some wings. I am going to actually make the unicorn tomorrow, hopefully it works!

Bye Diary!
PS I will get back to you about it tomorrow. I'm gonna call the unicorn a name like Cupcake!

Lauryn Wilkes (9)
Hazel Slade Primary Academy, Hazel Slade

Bleep Blop (An Alien)

Dear Diary,

Today was awesome and amazing! So today, Plob Pleeb woke me up, at who knows that time, by sneezing glitter into my face. I got out of my bed made of stars and went to get breakfast which was green milk and moon-shaped cereal. Since I live on the moon, I don't normally have visitors, so I decided to go back to bed for a bit and have a little snooze. Suddenly, Plob Pleeb started running around like crazy, throwing up rainbows everywhere! Plob Pleeb does that when she is nervous or worried, so I was quite scared as well! This giant rocket thing then landed on the moon and a weird human-like creature in a white suit with a fishbowl on its head came out of it. The human looked astonished when it saw Plob Pleeb and I. It came over to me. "Hello alien thing," it said, "You are famous on our land, especially your very rare species."

I felt amazed, thunderstruck, flabbergasted and stunned but enough about me. The human then showed me a box of cereal and a drink with my face on it!

I then fainted and woke up about twenty minutes later and wrote this! Plus, that weird human was gone!
Goodnight Diary, I'll write tomorrow!

Hollie Rachel Eileen Timms (10)
Hazel Slade Primary Academy, Hazel Slade

The Diary Of The Football Match

Thursday 14th March,

Dear Diary,

I couldn't believe it when our class teacher, Mr Mobberly, gave me the letter to go to the football match! The football match was against Littleton Green Primary School and we only had nine players. Thankfully, we've got Jayden and Ethan who are brilliant! I am looking forward to that match!

Friday 15th March,

Dear Diary,

Victory! We won four to three. Jordan gave the ball to me when it was one minute to the end and it was three to three, so I chipped the ball and it went on my head, so I headed it into the right-hand side of the goal. The crowd went wild! My mom whistled and my sister... *Wait,* I thought, *My sister was there! I thought she was at school!* Anyway, she screamed! The rest of the parents of Hazel Slade school cried, "Go Ezra, Go Ezra!"

Saturday 16th March,

Dear Diary,

What an amazing day! After all of the football game was over, everybody rushed to hug me (everyone apart from the parents of the other school that is), yes, everybody came! They queued and queued and queued! Now, that is all over. See you tomorrow!

Ezra Nathaniel Davies (8)

Hazel Slade Primary Academy, Hazel Slade

Katy Perry
An extract

17th June 2016,
Dear Diary,

I am so nervous! In five hours, I am going to Birmingham Arena to battle Taylor Swift. By battle, I mean to try and beat her at singing. Everyone is counting on me to win but I am still panicking! My make-up artist is coming to give me a makeover. Some other singers are coming to wish me luck, including Ava Max and Selena Gomez. I keep screaming a bit because my make up artist hasn't arrived yet. She is late... I don't know why I scream because it makes me more scared. What a terrible life I have. Oh, thank goodness, my make up artist has finally arrived and is doing my makeover. I can't believe it, my friends gave me a super cute outfit for the show. Of course, my friends are really helpful. My friends and I are now going out for dinner because I need to be on stage in two hours. I keep getting this feeling of 'what if something goes wrong'? After I finished dinner, I ate an apple pie for pudding, it was delicious. Now I am going to the studio to put my outfit on. My friends also gave me a hoodie with my name on!

Caitlan Haywood (8)
Hazel Slade Primary Academy, Hazel Slade

The Diary Of The Smelly Sock And The Golden Sock

Dear Diary,

A few days ago, I sat in the sock drawer with the golden sock. Bob then opened the sock drawer but he took the stripy pair and not me! The next day he didn't pick me! The next and the next and the next few days he didn't pick me, it went on for four days! Bob realised that he had an odd pair, so he chose my friend, the golden sock and me! He put us on swiftly and we went on a walk. We had so much fun. We went past some other socks, we had a rest on a beach as well. I could feel the foot was getting moist and I got really hot and sweaty. We then walked back home and we went past drowsy cows, quacking ducks, lonely meadows and blocks of flats. We took our boots off, well, Bob did, and we went slowly and drowsily up all the rickety stairs. We got put back into the sock drawer for the next exciting adventure but then Bob put us back on and went to the kitchen and got some crisps from the drawer.

Levi Brian Lees (9)
Hazel Slade Primary Academy, Hazel Slade

Bunny Wunny's Adventure

11th June, 11:09am,
Dear Diary,
You will never guess what happened today. My owner Niamh left me on the bed! It was so boring but then I fell and I was scared. I had never been down there before. I had better find a way back onto the bed, I'd better go.

11th June, 12:07pm,
Dear Diary,
It's impossible, I can't do it. I guess I can go and get some carrots from the kitchen.
Bye!

11th June, 12:10pm,
Dear Diary,
They're after me. How am I meant to get my carrots when these monsters are in the way... Oh, turns out they're the dogs but still, *argh!* Then I heard Niamh's mum. This was a disaster! I screamed for help but nobody heard me. My life was going to end.

12th June,

Dear Diary,

Turns out my life didn't end after all but it felt like it had. Niamh's mum had been getting her bag and had noticed me, so she called Niamh. We all went to Legoland and it was awesome. Good job she didn't forget me.

Niamh Boden (9)

Hazel Slade Primary Academy, Hazel Slade

One Punch Man

Dear Diary,

I had the best day ever because I killed lots of enemies in one punch and they were gone to where they belong, not in Heaven. There were a hundred and two of them, it took two seconds to kill them. Two seconds to kill forty-two of them with one punch. And then more came and I got all of them, all sixty of them. It was a bit hard but not really. Then I felt a hair pulled off my back. I turned around and it was there. The beast was... A little girl staring at me. I waited for it to strike and it did but I only got a scratch on my nose. I punched it and it just grew more heads. As class S and C came to help, I had to break the ball on its head. It took six and a half hours to kill and to get the ball out of its head. When I thought it was dead, it wasn't so I had to hit it once more.

Daniel Tonks (9)

Hazel Slade Primary Academy, Hazel Slade

The Incredible Diary Of...

Dear Diary,

Today I had a good day working as a monkey police officer. It was fun and exciting meeting new people and having jokes with people. I had to do cadet training which was very fun and very exciting. I fell in the mud once or twice which was fun. The monkey bars were the most fun because I am a monkey which is obvious because I am a pro with the monkey bars. They are easy to do because there are only twenty bars for me to climb. I did not fall into the mud but the next task I did was dreadful. it was the long jump. I hate the long jump because you have to jump over the mud but I fell into it, which was horrible. The mud was so wet and slimy. The mud felt like goo. The hardest thing was next, I had to climb up a house.

Harry Davis (9)
Hazel Slade Primary Academy, Hazel Slade

The Incredible Diary Of...

Dear Diary,

Today I went to a car show and it was amazing. I drifted and drifted and I went sliding. It was amazing, it was incredible because the wind was in my face and the windows protected my face from the mud, the grit and the tarmac from hitting my face. When I got home, I got my driver and went rally driving, it was amazing. I hit the roof again and it was just amazing.

Dear Diary,

Today I woke up and got my gear on and was ready to go. I am like the Stig because I have a white costume and I could be him. I raced the road in a forest with the music loud.

Callum Mottram (9)

Hazel Slade Primary Academy, Hazel Slade

Captain Adam The Spaceman

Dear Diary,

My name is Adam and I am a spaceman. I am travelling to a space station for my last day of training before the mission to Mars. Reuben, my brother, is also travelling with me and will be on the mission as well. We are training to fly the aircraft today.

Dear Diary,

After a day of training, we had to get our space food ready. I chose sandwiches, crisps, tomatoes and grapes with apple juice. Reuben chose wafers, crisps and pears. After choosing our food, it was time to get measured up for our spacesuits. After a busy day, we went to sleep at the space station at 5pm because we had to be up early.

Dear Diary,

This morning, I woke up early, put my spacesuit on and got my space food read. I loaded our robot, R2-D2, onto our spacecraft. I then went to wake Reuben up as he'd had a lie-in. We both then went to get in the spacecraft. We got off the spacecraft, ready for taking off and Reuben helped with the countdown.

Ten, nine, eight, seven, six, five, four, three, two, one, blast off!

Adam Thomas Albert Shepherd (9)

Horton Lodge Community Special School, Leek

Amazo Boy

An extract

Dear Diary,

Amazo Boy here, I can't tell you my real name but I will tell you this - it's pretty cool going through life as an actual superhero. What most kids dream of being. My father is Captain Atomic, the most awesome superhero in the galaxy. My mum is known as Speed Demon, she can run around the Earth in seven milliseconds. My sister is known as the Black Screamer, she has a supersonic voice and can destroy an animatron in just one blast, so we have to train her to use her powers carefully. Together, we are the superfamily, for good against evil. Even our pets have superpowers. I can tell you their names, our dog is called Barkey, also known as Ravager, he often helps Dad on his missions and his puppy-dog eyes can form a super force field, just with cuteness! He is also faster than Mum and can teleport to an ultimate dimension in just one minute. Our cat, Bibbles (it's a stupid name, I know) is also known as Wonderclaw. He can breathe fire, see in the dark and his claws are powerful enough to shred a hole in the fabric of reality. Bibbles also knows how to control it. Enough about my family for now...

Oli Halls (11)
Horton Lodge Community Special School, Leek

Caitlyn And Missy

Dear Diary,

It was a hot and sunny day and there was no school, yeah! I was wondering what to do when I looked down at Missy, my dog. I thought that I would walk Missy to the shops and have a cold drink on the way as it was a *very* hot day. I got in the powerchair, waved goodbye to my mum and dad and made my way down to the shops humming to myself, enjoying the weather with my dog. Then, oh my gosh, my chair ran out of all its power. I was wondering what to do when Missy barked up at me saying, "I will help you." Missy ran round the chair twice, very nutty, and I was scared as I didn't know what to do. Missy stopped then and became Toothless. She opened her mouth really wide and I saw a light building up fast and then it came out of her mouth. I was excited because I knew that it might help my chair get its power back. It didn't work on the first go, so she tried again but it still didn't work. Missy barked for help and you'll never guess what, the Light Furies came to help Toothless. They made light in their mouths, I could feel the heat and it was very hot.

They joined together and fired my chair back up. Toothless, the Light Furies and I went to get a cold drink. After that, we made our way home.

Caitlyn Butler (10)

Horton Lodge Community Special School, Leek

Alex

Dear Diary,

Today I am starting a new job as a brick-layer. I got out of bed and went to the building site. When I got there, I went to the boss' office and he told me to start laying bricks on a wall up to a ladder. The wall kept getting higher and higher, I was really enjoying my job. When I went to get a new pile of bricks, there were cubes. There were grey and green ones. I could now lay cubes really fast without moving my arms and if I made a mistake, I could delete them instantly. This was much easier than laying real bricks. Suddenly, a pig and a cow climbed up the ladder and started talking to me. It went dark really quickly and I saw a bed in the house, so I went to lie in it and went to sleep, waiting for the morning. I woke up in the night and saw blocky zombies and skeletons coming out of the ground. On the ground, there were sticks and cobblestones which turned into a pickaxe when I went to pick them up. Using the pickaxe, I smashed down the walls and climbed up the ladder. Then I heard someone shouting my name, it was my boss. He said, "Have you finished the wall already?"

Charlie George Taylor (7)
Hutchinson Memorial CE First School, Checkley

The Incredible Diary Of Coco The Rabbit

Dear Diary,

Today started just like any other normal day. Carrot, my brother, and I were chilling in our cages until four people came walking into the room. One little one came and looked right into my eyes and said, "Please can we have these two, Mum?"

We were scared and frightened, Carrot even ran to the back of the cage and hid! I was confident though, so I slowly moved a little closer. The other small person came over and stroked my nose. The mum of the two little ones got Carrot and I out of the cage and gave us a little box to sit in. After we were taken out of the box, we were put in a massive cage. It had an upstairs, downstairs and even a door to each room! This new home was way bigger than our last home. There was a huge feeding bowl full to the top with some water hanging up next to it.

As I had some refreshing water and a couple of bites of food, it started to rain. My new owners came running out of the house. They picked Carrot and I up and took us inside their house. First, we had a runaround, everything was so big!

Then we were put in smaller cages for the night, a bit like the first one we were in at the pet shop. Night-time was scary, we could hear strange noises and dogs howling. Carrot was hiding again.

Dear Diary,
We've been put back into the outdoor cage and because I had no sleep, I had a little nap. Carrot was upstairs eating.
Then the children came and let us out of our mini houses. We had a play in the garden while our owners cleaned our cages.
We had our dinner before having another play in the garden. This time was different, I was running around when suddenly two dogs came along. I played with them and we became best friends, whereas Carrot was really scared and hid behind me.

Dear Diary,
I've grown more and more confident with the dogs. Our cages are upgraded every month. I forgot about not being able to sleep at night and the weird sounds because I have been having so much fun.

Nancy Plant (9)
Hutchinson Memorial CE First School, Checkley

The Incredible Diary Of Billy Badger!

Dear Diary,

Today was strange. This morning when I woke up, around 5am, I was confused. It was Saturday and I had been with a boy called, Zack. He had a dog called Luna. Today we were meant to be going to a play centre but there were busy, so we went to Dimmingsdale instead to take Luna on a walk. When we arrived at Dimmingsdale, everyone got out of what they called a car and walked towards the wood. Zack was holding me by my chest so that I could see all the trees. It was fun, very fun indeed. Suddenly, out of nowhere, Luna ran and grabbed me by the tail and ran with me. Zack and his parents tried to stop Luna but it was no use, sadly. Luna stopped and started to sniff. She started to walk slowly, then a bit faster, then a bit faster until it felt like we were going 100 miles per second! Everything was a huge blur. Then she came to a stop, we were up a hill. Then she dropped me and ran away, then she came back with food in her mouth. Luna didn't notice me and kept on running.

When she was out of sight, I'd never felt so lonely in my life! I started to wander off towards some trees when nuts were being thrown at me. A squirrel came out of the tree and apologised. The squirrel said her full name was 'Nella Nutty Squirrel'.

I said that my name was Billy, Billy Badger. She asked me why I was out in the woods, so I told her and she said for me to follow her. So I followed her into her home. It was nice and cosy in there. She gave me a drink called mint tea in an acorn shell. It was yummy. She said, "Now you're filled up, let's go look for your owner."

I said, "He is only my owner for today and tomorrow." When we came out, I saw some dog prints, Luna's prints! We followed them, it took a while but eventually, we found Zack, Luna and his parents. *Yay!* We went back for tea and then we went to bed.

Bye, talk you to you tomorrow, Diary!

Daisy Armett (8)
Hutchinson Memorial CE First School, Checkley

Cody Mavric

Dear Diary,

Today I was having a great time playing football with my friends when all of a sudden, an owl swooped past and dropped a letter on my face. I opened the letter carefully and read it. It was a letter from Hogwarts! I didn't want my friends to see it because they didn't know I was magic, so I hid it in my pocket.

After running into the 9 3/4 wall, I realised that this wasn't Harry Potter. How could I get to Hogwarts? Suddenly, a homeless man appeared and offered me a whistle and whispered, "Wise choice, young Cody, I am Merlin. This whistle will call your transport." I blew the whistle and a Night Fury picked me up - it was a dragon!

When I got to Hogwarts, I was nervous and excited. I said goodbye to the Night Fury and entered the school. My first lesson was Quidditch. It was a match against Gryffindor! When I was playing, I saw the Golden Snitch. I chased it, hit it and it fell deep into the woods.

That evening, the moon shone bright, so I went to find the Golden Snitch. I was scared but it wasn't too much to handle. It was only a little trot into the woods. I found the Golden Snitch but I saw some toxic gas coming, so I ran to grab the Snitch and whistled for my dragon. He came very quickly.

Then Hidrascale appeared. Hidrascale is very evil. I gave the Golden Snitch to my dragon who ate it. He then gave a mighty roar and golden flames blasted out of his mouth, heading straight for Hidrascale. Hidrascale fell deep into the woods, hitting the ground. He sadly was never seen again. When I got back to my room, all the teachers were waiting for me. They were very surprised for it was only my first day and I had defeated the world's most powerful villain!

Tom Cooper (7)
Hutchinson Memorial CE First School, Checkley

Jackson's Disneyland Paris Experience

Dear Diary,

I am so excited I could burst, you'd never guess where I am going to! Oh yes, my whole family and I are going to Disneyland Paris! *Whoop, whoop!* We are travelling to London to catch the Eurostar over to Paris and can you believe it is happening all in the morning?

Dear Diary,

Well, the big day has arrived. We travelled to London and caught the Eurostar and I have now been in Paris for two hours. Upon my arrival, I couldn't contain my excitement for who met us at the hotel, it was only Mickey and Minnie Mouse! My heart missed a beat when I saw them, they are my most favourite Disney characters of all time. Minnie was wearing a red and white spotted dress and Mickey looked rather dapper in his gold bow tie. We had photos and a singalong, it was truly awesome. In the hotel, Winnie the Pooh was also in his tartan hat and coat with Tigger and Goofy. I felt like I was in heaven!

We had adventures planned to go around the Disneyland Parks to experience the flabbergasting rides. The Runaway Train was so fast I felt sick and 'It's a Small World' boat ride was just so dreamy, it slowed my heartbeat back to normal.

I couldn't believe my ears when I, Jackson Carr, was asked to be a part of the Disney Parade with Mickey and Minnie in their classic vehicle sitting in the back with them, all dressed up as a small Mickey Mouse, waving and clapping to the onlookers. All of my dreams had come true.

Anyway, must go now, Mum has just shouted me as we are going for dinner.

I will be back tomorrow with my next instalment of Jackson's Disneyland Paris experience.

Jackson Carr (9)
Hutchinson Memorial CE First School, Checkley

Gypsy The Dog

Dear Diary,

I woke up again at the kennels. My last owner abandoned me because I wouldn't stop barking. I was barking because I was starving and they wouldn't give me any food. They kicked me out and left me on the streets. Luckily, a big grey van came and took me to the kennels. They fed me and walked me but the other dogs were cruel to me. I felt lonely and was much older than everyone else. The people gave me some food and took me for a walk like they do every day. They opened the door so all the dogs could go outside. A woman came over to me and stared at me through the tall fence. I started getting really excited because it looked like she was going to adopt me. She talked to the people who owned the kennels, they opened the fence so that the woman could meet me and give me a stroke. She was really gentle and I loved her. Just as she looked like she was going to take me home, she got in her silver car and left. The people locked me back in the area where the other dogs were. Tears started to fill my eyes, I thought she would adopt me.

Dear Diary,

The woman has come back with a man and two little girls! The people who own the kennels came back and opened the fence. The woman, the man and the two little girls came over to me and stroked me. The people who owned the kennel gave the woman a lead and a collar. She put them on me and we all went to the silver car. The man and the woman lifted me into the car and took me home. They walked me, they fed me and treated me so much better than my old owners. I feel like my new owners all love me very much.

Verity Clark (9)

Hutchinson Memorial CE First School, Checkley

The Incredible Diary Of The Black Tiger

Dear Diary,

Today was a crazy day! I woke up in my sad and lonely bungalow. That moment, I felt like a spy. Suddenly the TV turned on and the news was the crown had been stolen and that the Queen was in the hospital. This was the opportunity to seize my moment, I would get the crown back! The thieves would be sorry about ever messing with me! I would seek out these maniacs and save the Queen! "I will never give up," I said to myself. I set off with my trusty car, 'Sally'.

I got all the murder weapons in 'Cluedo'. For six hours, I went out looking for shady characters. (There were quite a lot.) I saw lots of guys with tattoos, some were even going over the speed limit, very naughty!

Finally, I saw some activity. Six nerds were going into an abandoned building but they were just playing chess. I got roped into it too! It was nearly dawn, but I didn't stop for two more hours. I had to get some sleep though, I went back, disappointed. Five minutes later, I was sleepwalking but to my surprise, I was in a room full of diamonds and crystal jewels. I was the *best* thief in the world!

I am now known as the 'Black Tiger'. No one can ever stop me! I will be the world's biggest threat!

Harry Eccles (8)

Hutchinson Memorial CE First School, Checkley

Olivia Goodhew

Dear Diary,

Today hasn't been as good as I intended it to be. It all started when my dance teacher told me I was going to go on stage and show everybody what I had learnt. I was more ready than ever, I practised harder than I ever had before. Then the show started and I felt more nervous than ever before. Before I knew it, I was on the stage dancing the night away but then the most terrible thing happened. I tripped over and I had to be carried off stage. I couldn't dance anymore. I was so upset, I had practised so hard. It was so bad I couldn't stand up. I had to be taken to hospital.

A few hours later...
Dear Diary,

I've found out that I have a fractured ankle. The worst part is that I can't dance and I have to stay in hospital overnight.

A few days later...
Dear Diary,

I don't know what to do. I have played every single game in the world, I'm getting a bit bored. Luckily, the nurse came in and said that I can go home tomorrow. I am thrilled.

The next day...

Dear Diary,

They've told me that I'm all better and that I can go back to dancing. This is the best feeling in my life, the show can go on!

Olivia Goodhew (8)

Hutchinson Memorial CE First School, Checkley

Mohamed Salah

Dear Diary,

It is me, Mo Salah! Today has been amazing! We were in the FA Cup Final! Let me tell you about it. We kicked off at Wembley at 12pm. I was very nervous as we were playing Manchester City. They had the ball and we had to defend well, which we did. My teammates were on the counterattack. They passed it to me and I scored! 1-0, it was a good goal. The crowd were chanting my name. We were pressing. I had the ball, curled it and scored again! Could it get any better for me?
Half time: 2-0.

I had a quick drink and then we were off again. 2-1. We were poor at the back and let one in. It was the ninetieth minute and surely we would win. They had a final attack into the box and their man was tripped. Penalty - they scored it. The game was going to extra time.

A couple of minutes later, we won a free kick. It was the last minute of extra time. In came the cross. Someone headed it. It fell for me. I hit it and watched. It took a deflection, then it nicked the keeper and went in! I took my shirt off and everyone went crazy.

Full time, 3-2! I was the hat-trick hero!
We lifted the cup, what a day.

Noah Carr (8)
Hutchinson Memorial CE First School, Checkley

Steve And His Train

Dear Diary,

I woke up this morning because I remembered that it was the day I was taking my train to a festival. I quickly got out of bed and rushed my breakfast so that I could get my shiny train out. Bongo, my train, was looking spectacular in its apple-green livery as I'd painted it last night. I loaded Bongo carefully into my car and shot off to the festival. As soon as I arrived, I unloaded it slowly and lit the fire and got the pressure to 120PSI (pounds per square inch.) I went to get the coaches and then the people came and asked for a ride.

It was a very busy day and lots of people came to see Bongo. It was very exciting to see the happiness on the children's faces as they were riding a real steam train. Later that afternoon, I took the coaches off and gently steamed it down. Just then, when I noticed that it had steamed down, I gently put Bongo back in the car and went home. It was a lovely day and I was very tired.

Levi Morris (8)

Hutchinson Memorial CE First School, Checkley

Messi

Dear Diary,

For over a decade, I have been battling with Ronaldo to decide who is the best footballer in the world. This was decided at the match today, at the UEFA stadium. I have been practising all day and night. I was feeling a bit tired because I'd worked so hard.

We all played brilliantly. I was very proud of my team. It all came down to the last goal in the eighty-ninth minute. Mario Balotelli, a momentous player, fouled me inside the box. That meant it was a penalty and all eyes were on me. If I scored, we would win the match.

I slowly walked back to the edge of the box. I ran as fast as I could towards the ball, blasting it into the back of the net. It was like a rocket from outer space. It even made a hole when I shot it.

The match was over. I had won and Ronaldo had lost. I was feeling very happy. I was presented with my sixth Ballon d'Or trophy, showing I was the best footballer in the world!

Alex Holdham (8)
Hutchinson Memorial CE First School, Checkley

Olivia Keeling

Dear Diary,

Today I woke up at 12am to fly to Germany. We dressed and got into the van, ready to go to Stansted. It was a three-hour journey to the airport. I was so excited! When we got to the airport, it was about 3am. By the time we got through security and had a milkshake at the coffee shop, it was 4am. The milkshake was like a banana milkshake! By the time I had finished my milkshake, it was 5:40am and we all made our way to gate eighty-six. When we were boarding, it was 5:50am, in ten minutes we would be taking off to fly to Memmingen, Germany.

When we got to Memmingen, we caught a taxi to the train station. Once I got on the train we relaxed for an hour. When we got to Fischen, we found the block of flats. Then we unpacked our suitcases and went to sleep for half an hour. Then we went swimming until about 4pm.

After swimming, I had my tea and went to bed.

Olivia Keeling (8)
Hutchinson Memorial CE First School, Checkley

Tutankhamun

Dear Diary,

Earlier today I went on a walk to the fair with my dad. We went on lots of rides and had great fun. When we were on the dodgem cars, my dad spotted a beautiful girl called Ankhesenamun. He told me to spend the day with her and at the end of the day, to ask her to marry me. I was nervous to ask her and to talk to her. It took ages for me to pluck up my courage. Finally, I went over and asked her and guess what she said, she said yes! I nearly fainted. So I went over all the rides with her. There was the Mummy Cave, the dodgem cars and Beat the Pharoh. She loved to play Beat the Pharoh the best, whereas I didn't.

It was finally evening and I asked her to marry me. She said, "I wouldn't like to, I'd love to." It was the happiest day of my life. Then we got each other's number and went home.

Bye!

Tutankhamun, 10

Maisie Isabelle Weekes (8)

Hutchinson Memorial CE First School, Checkley

A Day In Candy Land

Dear Diary,

I had the best day *ever* today! After eating a delicious breakfast of candy-flavoured cereal, something out of this world happened. In a blink of an eye, I was in the sweetest land I'd ever seen. There was a chocolate flowing lake, mountains topped with whipped cream, trees with Mars bar trunks with colourful gummy bears hanging from each branch. My mouth was watering like a tap! As quick as a flash, I ran and dived into the soft, marshmallowy whipped cream head first! Not until I was feeling a bit sick did I get out to see what other sweet surprises I could find! I walked along a pebble path of milk chocolate buttons to find a field full of sheep with candyfloss fleeces! I saw a bench made of sponge cake and decided to sit down for a rest. Before I knew it, I was back in my kitchen and my cereal bowl was empty.
Was I daydreaming?

Lilly Bromage (8)
Hutchinson Memorial CE First School, Checkley

The Sea Dragon

Dear Diary,

Mummy and I went for a walk on the beach. I found a big blue egg hidden in the rocks while we were looking for shells. The dog chased the waves. We took all the bits we found back home. When I put the egg on the table, Mummy looked confused.

"Whoa, where did you find that?"

"At the beach."

It started to crack and crack and crack. It was a sea dragon. The dragon was hungry. I went downstairs to the cellar and looked in the fish cupboard and found a salmon.

After he ate the fish, I said, "We should go back to the beach because your mum should be there."

We took the dragon back to the beach. When he saw his mum, he licked me to say 'bye-bye' then he ran off to his mum.

I hope I will see him again.

Thomas Fallon-Bell (8)

Hutchinson Memorial CE First School, Checkley

Ed's Big Jewel

Dear Diary,

Today I had the craziest day of my life. I was on my way to the jewellery shop at 4:30am and I saw Officer Scout, so I hid in a rubbish bin. I got my glass cutter out and stepped in. I saw the most wonderful jewel, it was a red ruby! When suddenly, the alarm went off. I grabbed the ruby and ran to my apartment. Officer Scout saw me and shot me with his taser.

"Arrgh!" I shrieked. Officer Scout got attacked by a pigeon as I broke free. I didn't expect that to happen. I limped as fast as I could to my apartment. I grabbed my suitcase and packed it up to the brim. I will have to flee to another country because I am now at five-star wanted level. Who knows, this time next year I could be writing from jail...

Archie Clacher (8)

Hutchinson Memorial CE First School, Checkley

The Incredible Diary Of Clint Eastwood

Dear Diary,

Today I was shot, so I shall tell you how it started. I was getting up this morning and I went to get my men. Their names were Billy the Kid, John Wayne and Nicholas. When I woke them up, they told me a brand-new town had opened in Hill Valley. I set off and on the way, I met a few gangsters. Suddenly they shot John Wayne and then I shot them back. In the distance I did not notice the sheriff, he was a very ugly sheriff. He shot me in the leg but it did not kill me. I played dead and then my friends and I killed him. When I finally got there, I went into the saloon and I got a few whiskeys. We set up camp early because we were having rabbit for dinner.

Today was my favourite day, aside from being shot.

John-Curtis Price (8)
Hutchinson Memorial CE First School, Checkley

199

Mario

Dear Diary,

Something really strange happened. I was playing Super Mario Odyssey on my Nintendo. Suddenly, I got sucked into the game and I became Mario. It was amazing! Bowser and Peach were there. I had to defeat Bowser at the castle on the moon, so I set off in my spacesuit. I took huge spacemen steps to get there. It was so much fun to jump and float in space.

Bowser was waiting for me. We had a ferocious battle and for a moment, I thought I was going to lose but at the last minute, I won. Bowser was defeated. Peach asked me to take her to the Mushroom Kingdom, so we flew to the Mushroom Kingdom. All of a sudden, I found myself back in my mum's car playing on my Nintendo!

Henry Charles William Minshall (7)
Hutchinson Memorial CE First School, Checkley

What A Day!

Dear Diary,

Today was a nerve-wracking day because it was a gymnastics competition. My legs felt like jelly and I had never been to a gymnastics competition before. Today was the day, as soon as I got there, I took a deep breath and did what I had to do. I leapt onto the vault and ended into a straddle stand. At the end of the competition, my name was called, I'd won three medals and three trophies. I was so happy that I'd won the vault, beam and floor. I rushed home to show my mum and dad my awards. What a day!

Ruby Foster (7)

Hutchinson Memorial CE First School, Checkley

Me And My Cat!

Dear Diary,

My cat, Ellie, was lost. Her brother Max was very sad as they are twins. We looked through the fields and then the garden but the sheep and goats hadn't seen her. Max and I walked all over the farm calling her name, even the dogs couldn't help. It was only at night feed when mummy went to get the quad bike that she found Ellie. She had been asleep on an old blanket in the workshop, she couldn't understand what the fuss was about! But she doesn't understand how much we love her!

Isabelle Wibberley (7)

Hutchinson Memorial CE First School, Checkley

The Day I Met A Dino

Dear Diary,

Today was rather weird but wonderful and also unbelievable. Now, this is how it all began...

When I woke up, it was a pretty ordinary day and I was doing my make-up, I am Candice of course, you know me, I'm obsessed with make-up. Anyway, my mum came into my purple palace of a room and said, "Open your blinds, you can't waste electricity!" So I did as I was told and opened my blinds, but to my utter surprise, there outside of my window, was a dinosaur! This couldn't be real could it? Starstruck, I gathered most of my belongings and raced downstairs, straight into the garden. It was real, it was actually there! Suddenly the purple and green dino grabbed onto me. I was petrified. Where would it take me and why? The dino ran and ran and then she started to fly! "Argh," I screamed from up high. At that moment, I felt scared and confused.

A few minutes later, I started to notice that we were heading back down to land but it did not look like Earth or space, it looked like a new world. Eventually, we got down to land. I was in some sort of mansion made of rocks!

Harriet Faith Hosell (9)
St Joseph & St Theresa RC Primary School, Chasetown

My Time Flying Disaster

Dear Diary,

The most unusual thing happened to me today. I was strolling along the beach when suddenly I saw an old-fashioned pocket watch. Its cracked, broken face reflected the light. I stopped and stared. Why was it here? Where had it come from? Was it ancient? Quickly I rushed over to it. *Is it safe?* I thought. Slowly but carefully I picked it up and looked closely. I twisted the handles. As I did, something felt strange around me. It suddenly got really foggy and I couldn't see a thing.

When the fog cleared, I was in the Jurassic time! I got really scared because the bushes were moving. What was there? Hesitantly I said, "H-h-h-hello?" Two red beady eyes appeared in the bush. Cautiously I turned round then... ran as fast as my legs would carry me.

As I was running I looked behind me and saw a menacing smile with eyes as dark as blood. All of a sudden it swooped down beside me and showed me its evil talons.

Luckily, out of nowhere, a T-rex came and saved me. He opened his mouth and showed his dagger-like fangs. *What should I do? Quick, think! Ah ha!* I pulled out my watch and as quick as I could twisted the handles and *boom!*

204

I was in the 17th century. It was the Great ire of London! Golden flames jumped from roof to roof, intense black smoke separated me from everyone. The flames, which were as bright as the sun, came to gobble me up. The scorching heat surrounded me. I couldn't take it anymore so I twisted the clock some more.

I was in the future! All of a sudden, silence fell in the crazy town. Robots and aliens started coming towards me. *Twist, twist.* "Please take me home!" When the fog had cleared it was a relief to see my family again.

I was glad to be home!

Lily Fryer (10)

St Joseph & St Theresa RC Primary School, Chasetown

The Dancing Queen

An extract

Dear Diary,

This weekend was unreal! It started off like this: I collected my dance partner, Lilly. Lilly is sunny, funny and cute, just like a little bunny. She has short, honey blonde hair and the prettiest eyes. We did our handshake, gave each other a hug and jumped in the car and off we went! It was a short journey to the competition, hoping the next day that I'll get recognition. Once we got there, I opened the car door and it felt like I had walked into a freezer. In the distance, there was a glistening, sparkling ice tower. As I got closer, it looked like someone had pressed 'pause' on the remote control because the water was playing musical statues. As Lilly and I walked through the dark, lonely corridors, we heard a rumbling sound. We came to a large wooden door with big black writing: *Ballroom.* I grasped the door handle with the palm of my sweaty, warm hands and nervously pulled open the door. *Bang!* The sound hit me like a train. There were hundreds of people, dancers, parents, dance teachers and judges all shouting above the din of the music.

Over the next two hours, Lilly and I danced our fast solos, rock 'n' roll and fast pairs, we did well! But what was to come was why I was really here - the slow dance. I danced from my heart, the best I could, luckily getting through to the final! Thinking about it now makes me tingly!

In the final, I had to dance on my own in front of seven dragon-like judges. Lights off, spotlight on, just me and the dance...

Tayla Mae Ewen (9)

St Joseph & St Theresa RC Primary School, Chasetown

Scary But Fun In Disney World!

Dear Diary,

I was inside the Disney World Park in the haunted warehouse. I was super nervous! It scared me so much that I ran out. There was a flash of lightning and no one was at the park. It was terrifying! I went to go and look around but I couldn't see anyone apart from six nightmare characters, one in a pumpkin suit, one in a witch's costume, one in a skeleton costume, one in a mummy suit, another in a werewolf costume and the last in a zombie dog costume which was actually cute. They came up to me and I screamed. I ran at the same time as they started chasing after me like a bunch of cheetahs. We went past so many rides. I was running out of breath, I quickly and quietly had to hide. I had a quick drink. They were there, right in front of me. They took their masks off and in the pumpkin costume was Mickey Mouse, in the witch's costume was Minnie Mouse, in the skeleton costume was Donald Duck, in the mummy suit was Daisy Duck, in the werewolf costume was Goofy and Pluto was in the zombie dog costume.

We all had fun together in the end and we went on so many rides.
Speak to you tomorrow!

Rhiannon Thomas (8)

St Joseph & St Theresa RC Primary School, Chasetown

Unicorn Magic Goose Chase

Dear Diary,

I am on my way to London and I can see a rainbow in the sky. What could it mean? I'm very excited to get into London!

Dear Diary,

As you know I am on my way to London and I have seen a rainbow. Our mum said that we had arrived. I saw the beautiful house that I could only describe as extraordinary, amazing and awesome. All of a sudden, my mum opened the door and the walls were painted in rainbow colours. After we brought the things inside, we went to Buckingham Palace. We saw the Queen but it was weird because the Queen stood out in the middle of her garden.

Suddenly, I saw her stamp and the rainbows started to come to her and a unicorn came out. The Queen jumped onto the unicorn and then I stepped forward and stepped on a stick. The unicorn heard me and it started running around and then it went straight through Buckingham Palace and out of the door.

The Queen was screaming because she was on the back of it. The Queen's guards were chasing after her. The guards got the unicorn and the rainbow came again and picked the unicorn up and took it back to where it belongs.

Ava (8)

St Joseph & St Theresa RC Primary School, Chasetown

The Day I Could Not Stop Dreaming

Dear Diary,

On Friday night when I was lying in my bed, I started to dream about a noise coming from my attic. So I went to investigate. I tiptoed as quietly as I possibly could. I reached for the brown, wooden attic ladders and opened the attic doors. Then I heard a whimpering sound. In the corner of the attic, I saw an object so I went over and saw an idy-bidy green metallic alien crying. So I whispered, "What are you?"

The green metallic alien answered, "I crashed down here and lost my parents."

I said, "Don't worry, I will help you get home."

The small alien muttered, "Okay."

Just then, I saw another one of these objects. Then I remembered it was a spaceship and it had small people inside who were waving to the small alien. Then the alien bellowed, "Mommy, Daddy!"

Then I realised that it was all a dream and Mommy was shouting, "Frankie, Frankie, wake up!" I felt like I had never been asleep.

Lilliemai Brookes (10)
St Joseph & St Theresa RC Primary School, Chasetown

The Shark Attack

Dear Diary,

You will never guess what I saw a few days ago. I saw the most terrifying thing ever, a shark chasing somebody!

It looked like the shark was getting closer and everybody could see this, we all wondered if the man would survive or not.

All of a sudden, the man got faster but so did the shark. They were still so far into the sea that we couldn't see the shark, only his fin. Every second, it seemed to get faster and the man was swimming as fast as he could. They looked like they were five hundred metres away.

Then they looked as though they were fifty metres away. The man finally reached the shore and as he climbed out of the water, somebody shouted, "Watch out, watch out!" but the shark had managed to bite both of the man's legs off. Everyone got the man a wheelchair.

After that, the authorities said that it looked like it had been a killer shark and that it was ten metres long. That was crazy.

I'll write again soon.

Luke Thomas James Tann (8)
St Joseph & St Theresa RC Primary School, Chasetown

The Dinocat And The Queen

The year, 4019.

Dear Diary,
I am the queen. I had a terrible dream about a horrible dinosaur and he roared, "Give me a marshmallow, you old hairy bear."
I thought I was dreaming and I was, I rang my bell and my servant came upstairs and gave me a bagel, a hot chocolate and a newspaper. I ate my breakfast and told her my dream. She said that I should read the newspaper on the very first and second page. I did ask her why but she didn't respond. So I read the newspaper and it was the same as my dream, a horrible greedy dinosaur wanted all the food in the universe! I fainted for an hour, I was extremely shocked.
I came outside. "Hello, give me some goodies," said a big, deep voice. Everyone screamed and everyone ran away but my servant and I stared in complete silence. The dinosaur started to cry but we calmed him down. He asked for some food, so we had a picnic.
I will write again soon.

Mia Elizabeth Hall (7)
St Joseph & St Theresa RC Primary School, Chasetown

Rock Star Royals

Dear Diary,

You will be astonished when I tell you what I witnessed today! It was the most astonishing thing that has ever happened to me!

I have a younger brother and two sisters who stayed at Gran's house while Mum and Dad took me to London. We had arrived at our flat when Mum said to me, "Why don't you go for a walk and get some fresh air." I didn't argue and just left the small, dusty room muttering to myself. As I passed by Buckingham Palace, I saw something I will never forget.

I saw the Queen but she wasn't all dainty and prancing around the palace, she was running around with other people. She had an electric guitar in her hand. She was in a secret gang of royal rock stars! I just knew I had to tell someone but I also knew that I shouldn't let the Queen down, so here I am telling you, Diary.

I have enjoyed writing to you, I'll see you soon!

Juliet (8)

St Joseph & St Theresa RC Primary School, Chasetown

Best Day Ever!

Dear Diary,

Today was incredible! I woke up to a note that said: 'Meet me in the kitchen'. So I went and got dressed, it was Mum and Dad, they said, "Come and get in the car."

I said, "What for?"

Dad said, "It's a surprise!"

I said, "Let's go"

"Great idea," said Dad.

So we went and I could see a sign that said *Pet Shop.* I felt happy, joyful and excited. Oh no, the car had stopped! I was worried about what might happen. We could see my nan next to us, so she drove us there. I could see all of the animals, so I asked my mum what we were getting and she said, "A dog!" I could have screamed, I was so happy. We got a doggy and she is so cute. We went home and I played and played with her. Then we all went on a walk. Then we went to bed.

Phoebe Sherwin (9)

St Joseph & St Theresa RC Primary School, Chasetown

Amazing Super Girls

You won't guess what I saw outside my window. I saw a group of superheroes attacking a scary, freaky monster. I was amazed.

I rushed outside and asked them, "Who are you?" They told me their names: Polly, Lucy, Emily and Poppy the leader. "We're attacking a monster."

I said, "I can see that."

"We better get back to work."

"Wait, can I help?"

Poppy said, "Yeah sure." Luckily she'd brought a net. Poppy said, "Let's throw the net over its head and then use our magic to turn it to stone." So they did. I went back to their house and we had a party. I said, "Do you always celebrate?"

"Yes," said Poppy.

And that was the end of my very exciting but unusual day!

Iris Winifred Bladon (7)

St Joseph & St Theresa RC Primary School, Chasetown

The Terrible Sleepover

Friday 8th March 2019.
Dear Diary,
My friend India had a sleepover at my new house in the dark, scary woods. I don't know why we were even sleeping at my house as it is that creepy.
At midnight, we heard a very creepy scream coming from my wardrobe as it started to shake. We were speechless...
We went into my mum and dad's room, they went into my room and searched the whole place. We went back to my room and there was something that was not there before.
There were dolls' heads and spiders all on my bed. India said, "I think we should look inside the wardrobe."
I replied, "Okay, let's do it." Mum and Dad were hiding in the wardrobe, they'd done it all!
India and I went back to bed, I hope it won't happen again.

Daisy Elizabeth Mee (7)

St Joseph & St Theresa RC Primary School, Chasetown

Weird Horse One, Weird Horse Two

Dear Diary,

You will never guess what I did and what I saw today. It was somewhere unexpected as well...

I heard a weird noise coming from the school forest, so I went to see what it was. My spine tickled and it was a herd of horses! OMG! So cute. I wondered if I could ride on one of them. Uh-oh, I heard a thunderstorm. A strike of lightning hit a horse, oh no!

I saw a horse lying down next to the dead one. That horse looked kind of stupid. I really thought it was but it wasn't. It was bringing the dead horse to life and it gave it wings? Wait, what? But how... I thought I was going to faint!

I rode on its back.

Well Diary, that is it for today because I am really tired. So night, night Diary! I will write in you again tomorrow.

Leah Burke (8)

St Joseph & St Theresa RC Primary School, Chasetown

The Alien Invasion

Dear Diary,

You will never guess what happened last night. Whilst I was in my bed I saw a light outside. It was red, in fact as red as fire. I didn't know what it was. I was terrified.

About six minutes later there was screaming. I looked out the window. No one was there, nothing. This was a mystery, a big mystery. I closed the curtain and checked again. Still nothing.

I was waiting for a while, seeing if there was going to be more screaming. Another thirty minutes later the screaming came back! "What's happening? Am I in a dream?" I said.

Suddenly it became louder. Why? Then it was midnight. I checked the curtain and there was an alien!

All of a sudden I was in bed, it was morning. What happened?

Alfie Dixon-Smith (8)

St Joseph & St Theresa RC Primary School, Chasetown

The Incredible Diary Of...

Dear Diary,

Today was the weirdest day ever! First, the head teacher banned maths. It was great! The teacher took us on a picnic, we ate cake, chocolate, sandwiches, muffins and cupcakes. Then an ice cream van came and we were all excited! Except for Lucas Learn who loved maths!

When we came back, there was a dog the size of a skyscraper, he was standing on the roof of the school, he was about to break the roof when we saw police lights! They shot a net that flew over the top of our heads, shaved the roof and missed him! He put his foot down and crushed the school and destroyed the textbooks. Lucas Learn was practically ripping his hair out now. Then the dog shrank because the head teacher shot the dog with her laser eyes.

Kacper Piotr Lis (10)

St Joseph & St Theresa RC Primary School, Chasetown

Dreaming Of A Unicorn! I Think?

Dear Diary,

You will never guess what I did and what I saw today. I was pulled into a world I never quite believed in, it was really weird. I was in a forest, so it was really risky.

Suddenly, I heard a really strange sound coming from further on in the forest, I was going to investigate what it was but I was too scared but then I saw some footsteps. There was a herd of horses! The footsteps kept on leading me to the herd of horses. All of a sudden, I saw something running with the herd of horses and it had a horn...

Suddenly, I was in my bed and I was not in the big forest. I did not understand at all. Was it a dream? Hopefully, this won't happen again. I think it was a unicorn!

I will write again soon.

Bria Webster-Ayre (7)

St Joseph & St Theresa RC Primary School, Chasetown

The Trip To London!

Dear Diary,

On Thursday morning, I went to school and I did my work. At the end of the day, the teacher had said that we were going on a trip to London! I rushed home and said, "Mum, I'm going on a trip to London! I can't believe it! I'm too scared!" "Okay, okay," my mum had said.

Dear Diary,

On Friday morning, I was so confused, I said to myself that I would take my iPhone with me, my real one. After a while, I arrived at school and the bus was already there. We went on the bus and it drove us to London. When we arrived, I saw the Queen! The Queen was walking down the street. We had lots of fun there. We were there for three hours. I took a picture of the Queen.

Marika Orlinska (8)

St Joseph & St Theresa RC Primary School, Chasetown

What A Bummer

Dear Diary,
Tomorrow it's my birthday and I am turning ten. I am really curious to see where we go. Last year we went to the beach but I think we're going on holiday where trees dance and praise me.

Dear Diary,
When I woke, my family dragged me into the car saying, "We are going to a fair!" When I heard those words, I was upset, I thought this was going to be the worst birthday ever but it ended differently. When we got there, it was full of zombies. We were tied up and later on, we saw more zombies who asked us if we could be best friends. We said yes and they gave us a real unicorn, we were surprised. What will happen next...?

Ria Thomas (9)
St Joseph & St Theresa RC Primary School, Chasetown

The Scary School

Dear Diary,

You will never guess what happened to me! I was kicked into a different world of scary things.

As you know, I had moved schools and I had been hearing people saying 'help me' at this one but I'm wasn't sure why. I had gone to the toilet and washed my hands when water shot out and made a gaping a hole. I stepped closer and saw talking toys, weird slime stuff and all sorts.

I could still hear someone saying, "Help!" I clenched my hands and said to myself that it wasn't really happening but then I wondered if it was...

Suddenly, I was back in my warm bed.

William Cunningham (8)

St Joseph & St Theresa RC Primary School, Chasetown

Little Mermaid Friends

Dear Diary,

Hi, I'm Princess Kate. I live in a castle with my friend, Princess Sarah the Second. My family moved out seven years ago. I am twenty-seven and Princess Sarah is twenty-four years old. Something has happened that I can't explain... I saw a necklace under my bed. I got it from under my bed so I could see it better. I put it on...

Once I had put it on I turned into a shiny, rainbow-tail mermaid. I was scared and I was in the ocean. Then I saw my friend Princess Sarah. She did not have a necklace but she was a mermaid!

I will write again soon!

Emilia Silk (7)

St Joseph & St Theresa RC Primary School, Chasetown

The UFO World

Dear Diary,

You will never guess what happened? A UFO was on top of the school, it was so scary. We were all running to the classroom but the bright lights were there.

The next morning, there were big banging sounds on my window. Then I heard a tapping on the roof. Afterwards, I opened my curtains and there was a huge alien dog but he was a good dog. I let him in but he made a huge noise.

Later that morning, my mum woke up and she said, "You've met my old dog, I love him."

We let him in go in the end.

I will write to you soon!

Sienna (8)
St Joseph & St Theresa RC Primary School, Chasetown

The Mysterious Dream

Dear Diary,

You will never guess what happened last night. I heard a creepy noise whilst I was asleep.

I suddenly heard a noise and it sounded like it was coming from under my bed and then I heard a tapping noise coming from my bedroom door.

I woke up and first looked under my bed but there was nothing under there. Then I checked outside my bedroom and there was also nothing there. Then, I heard a crunching noise which I thought was coming from the driveway. I rushed to my window but this time, I saw a car pulling up on the driveway...

Oliver Davies (8)

St Joseph & St Theresa RC Primary School, Chasetown

Creaky Bed

Dear Diary,

The other night I was sleeping in my bed when I heard a sound. I hid under my bed covers and then I heard some footsteps. I was home alone that night!

When I woke up later that day, I went downstairs and got breakfast but it looked mouldy, as did the milk, so I didn't have any.

Then I went under my bed but I saw a monster. I screamed as loud as I could, "Help, help!" but no one came. The monster did go away for a while but then it came back and it happened again!

Jescie Lindsey (8)
St Joseph & St Theresa RC Primary School, Chasetown

The Scary Creature

Dear Diary,

You would not believe it, I am in a terrifying house. It is a dark and spooky house. Earlier today, I heard footsteps coming up my stairs and I hid under my cover. It was so scary.

Then my cupboard door started to open and shut. I shouted for my mum and dad but they didn't answer. I walked around and I saw a skeleton on the floor. There was also blood on the floor in a trail. I followed the trail and found my mum and dad dead!

I will write again soon.

Ella Hanslow (8)

St Joseph & St Theresa RC Primary School, Chasetown

Circus Funtasia

Dear Diary,

Today I went to the Circus Fantasia with my mum. We saw lots of different circus acts, some were really scary and I wondered if they would get hurt. It made my stomach feel weird. There were four motorbikes whizzing around a humongous wire ball. They were very close together, they could've been hurt.

After the circus, we went to Pizza Hut and we had a ham and pineapple pizza and chips. *Yum.* We had a really nice day.

Alice Ansell (10)

St Joseph & St Theresa RC Primary School, Chasetown

The Biting Dogs

Dear Diary,

You will never guess what has happened to me! I went to a cricket game. Someone batted the cricket ball so high that it went into someone's garden! I went into the garden and I got the ball but there were dogs! The dogs were chasing me like I was a bone. The dogs bit me to death...

The next thing I knew, I was in the hospital and no one knew where I was...

I will write again.

Rhyan Hamilton (8)

St Joseph & St Theresa RC Primary School, Chasetown

Creepy Dream

Dear Diary,

I was at school and I saw a light shining on the playground.

I started to shake. What was happening? I heard some noises but I decided to ignore them, but I was too distracted. Suddenly, I saw a spooky bright UFO land. *Ow! My eyes*, I thought. Then the noise got louder and louder. I then saw an alien. I thought, *wow! Is this all a dream?*

Zackery (8)

St Joseph & St Theresa RC Primary School, Chasetown

Ellie And Her Vacation Adventure

An extract

Dear Diary,

I can't believe I've got my first ever diary! *Eek!* OMG! I was just about to say goodnight to you but Mum came in saying that there is a surprise waiting for me tomorrow, I can't wait so I need to go to sleep.

Night!

7th August 2018,

Dear Diary,

Good morning, I almost forgot what my mum had told me about the surprise until I saw Mum waiting by my door holding a holdall, tickets and a suitcase. In the room, there were two bags that held things like food and snacks. Mum said, "Wake up you lazy potato! Get dressed into something warm and comfy because we're going to visit Uncle John." OMG! I was so excited! I couldn't write in my diary on the plane because I was being a lazy potato! So I have already arrived and I'm going to bed, goodnight!

8th August 2018,

Dear Diary,

Today was my first day in England, I could already smell the English breeze and hear the kettle screaming. I got dressed quickly and rushed to the kitchen where Uncle John was waiting since he told me he will show me around the place. We all ate breakfast and headed out. It was a very foresty place but I quite liked it. At the end of our little road trip he showed me a wonderful place called Greenfield Stables that was filled with beautiful horses. All of them looked stunning but there was this one horse that stood out to me, his name was Bailey. It was getting late, so we needed to get back home and head to bed. After lunch, which was really late, we all headed to our rooms and plonked into bed but I wasn't tired because I couldn't stop thinking about the beautiful horses but after all that, I did fall asleep.

Martyna Anna Denis (10)

St Modwen's Catholic Primary School, Burton-On-Trent

Superstar Singing School Competition

Dear Diary,

Another miserable Monday, I dragged myself out of my cosy bed, slumped myself at the dining table where Mum had cooked me a fabulous breakfast. "Look what your friend, Khaziama, left for you," Mum said eagerly. I ran to the door and picked up the envelope Khazi had left. *What is it?* I thought to myself. As I opened it, I saw a glimpse of the word 'singing'... I was so excited. "Khaziama, you're the best!" I shouted at the top of my voice. Then I ran into the kitchen and told my mum about the competition. "You'd better start practising," Mum whispered quietly.

I ran to my room and started practising my singing. Hours went by, my voice grew sore but I continued because I wanted to win the competition.

I woke up on the morning of the competition and I went to shout good morning to my brother but nothing came out. *I've lost my voice, what shall I do?* Panic set in. *What shall I do?* I quickly brushed my teeth, then I went downstairs as fast as I could! I was trying to say something but nobody was listening.

While I was having breakfast, I was thinking about what had happened. Then Khazi came to know if I was ready. Khazi noticed that my voice was gone, Khazi gave me some yummy tea and honey. Suddenly, my voice came back and I was ready for the show. I was dressed as a pretty girl, everyone said I looked fabulous. When we got there, I waited for my go. Finally, it was my turn, I thought I'd blown it but it was amazing. In the end, the results came and I was in the first place! It was so cool, I got my price of £500 and a medal.

Catherin Sijoy (9)
St Modwen's Catholic Primary School, Burton-On-Trent

The Ridiculous Road Trip

Dear Diary,

Today I had a mixed feeling day! At one point of the day, I was bored, angry, frustrated and mad but at the other part of the day, I was happy, excited, joyful and glad. So let me tell you the story. We were basically just getting ready to go in the car to go to Disney Land. My dad was getting our bags and suitcases in the car while my mum, my grandmas, my two annoying brothers and I were getting in the car. After ten minutes of fuss and arguing over who was sitting where we finally set off! Then, because we'd had no breakfast and we were literally starving, we went to the KFC drive-thru. It was a bit gross because we got sticky sauce all over the seats and some French fries landed on the dirty floor but it was better than nothing! So after everyone was full, we started driving. I was very bored because I'd forgotten my iPad was in my backpack in the boot but when we stopped to have some fresh air, I got it then. When we were halfway there, my dad's car broke down! My dad tried to fix it but it wouldn't do. I was kind of scared because I had waited to come here all year. After what seemed like an hour, a man parked by us and started asking questions like, "What's happened?" and "Where are you going?"

My dad started talking to him and soon after he shouted, "Get the bags out and get in the car!" Everybody did as we were told, the kind man drove us to Disneyland! We got into our hotel room and had some dinner. Then I got into my PJs and watched TV. I probably wouldn't go to sleep today.
Signed,
Debby Goldstar

Hanna Motas (9)
St Modwen's Catholic Primary School, Burton-On-Trent

The Incredible Diary Of Kaede

An extract

Dear Diary,

Kaede here! Funny news, I'm stuck. Yeah, I got into this weird reality show that puts you against fourteen other people your age, no big deal. Well, apart from the fact that we do challenges and the last one out of their challenge room gets stuffed into a robot, there's no big deal. But look on the bright side, I'm not dead! I also found someone that I think I think I'm in love with. don't tell anyone though, even if you can't move. Anyway, his name is Shuichi and he's *adorable!* Yet I have a feeling someone else likes him... Her name is Miu and she's a good friend of mine, so it's hard to hate her. You know what? Let's get off the topic of love and talk about this show. The first thing is that the show is hosted by a shady guy in a hood. the second thing is that we don't have our phones. can you believe it? Third and final thing, he makes us wait in some empty room once we finish the challenges. How do I know this? Well, I finished the first challenge. It was about solving a murder scene, it turns out a robber shot himself so the police couldn't catch him. It was really dark, mysterious and blood filled in that room.

I managed to get out in a second and a small fifteen-year-old got placed into a robot. His name was Kibo, now its K-1-Bo. Another boy, his best friend, had left second to last. His name was Kokichi.

Oh, now we are going to the second challenge! Got to cut this short,

Kaede out!

Alexis Mabatid (10)

St Modwen's Catholic Primary School, Burton-On-Trent

Runaway Princess

An extract

Dear Diary,

This morning I was reading my favourite book as usual when my mother came into my room and said, "What are you doing in here, you're supposed to be with your father practising your speech for the Gaurdners of Lavatica."

You must be wondering what Lavatica is, well it's basically the country which I might rule over someday. You guys might think it's a dream come true but sorry to burst your bubble, it isn't a dream come true. You have to follow strict rules and use your manners, even if it's only for family dinners, and you have to wear perfect shoes, perfect gowns, perfect accessories and perfect everything but the only rule that is the strictest is that you are not allowed to go outside the castle without any guards. I live a boring life most of the time, but my best friends, Fesebelle and Vidego, are the best friends you could ever ask for. After dinner, I was lying on my bed wondering what boring things I have to do tomorrow when an idea popped up in my head which changed my life forever. The idea of me running away from my castle. I didn't know if I was crazy or not but I stuck to my idea.

I had a feeling that if I went alone, the moment I stepped out I would be as scared as a chicken. So I called my friends to come with me, they were totally up for this idea. We made a plan to leave the castle at midnight and to run away...

Maria Mathew (9)
St Modwen's Catholic Primary School, Burton-On-Trent

Pele, Zero To Hero

Dear Diary,

Today was a really big day for me. I was in the dressing room getting changed into the Brazil kit. The pressure was on to make our country proud and to win our first world cup. I was really nervous but I was really excited at the same time. We were against Sweden, we were in Sweden so they had the advantage. It was a really good game until Sweden got the ball and scored by Nils Liedholm which got our heads down but we played on until the end. All of a sudden, we came with a reply, Vava scored to make the score 1-1 and it was equal. We played really nicely and Sweden did as well.

Then came another goal from my teammate Vava who scored another goal and he was having a fantastic game. The score was 1-2. This meant that we were winning and I was so happy that we were. After that, I had the ball and kicked it over the defender, shot and scored. I was over the moon that I had scored because it was a huge achievement. Then we scored another one by Mario Zagallo, the score was now 1-4. Then Sweden scored and it was 2-4, then at the last moment, I scored again and it was 2-5.

Then the whistle blew and we won our first World Cup as we celebrated on the pitch. We were so happy and relieved because we got the 1958 World Cup! I enjoyed the moment, looking at that piece of gold.

Ben Jacob (10)

St Modwen's Catholic Primary School, Burton-On-Trent

My Horrible And Mysterious Day

Dear Diary,

I was so late for school today. Damn it. I was told off by my horrible teacher, Miss Evers. She has short grey hair on a wrinkly, miserable face and I absolutely hate her.

By the way, I'm Ashley Harrison and I live at thirty-three Greenway Lane. Anyway, I'll catch you later, right now I've got to go.

Dear Diary,

School was terrible! I only got three out of ten on my maths test. You can't blame me though because maths is *so* hard. That's not all, I missed my break because I was 'messing around' with my best friend, Laura Jane. I couldn't help talking to her in the middle of a boring history lesson about Vikings.

You would think that this is the worst that could happen but it wasn't. I was walking past the grand, ancient chapel and then thirty-one... thirty-two... and thirty-three Greenway Lane but something was wrong!

The cheerful, bright red door of my homely, welcoming house was already swung open and the beautiful blue doormat was covered in grubby black marks. This could only mean one thing, someone had snuck in! My heart was racing, I was terrified and worried but I had to investigate...
See you later,
Love from,
Ashley.

Annmiya Tharappel (10)
St Modwen's Catholic Primary School, Burton-On-Trent

The Magical Animal

Dear Diary,

Today I saw two girls that went to the woods. As they went through, they saw a lost animal. The two girls felt a bit worried but they knew that they could help. So they took the animal to the vet so that the vet could look after it. Then they found out that it was not a normal dog, it was a magical dog that made wishes come true, and then the dog grew some wings that were big and sparkly. One of the girls said that she would like to have thousands of sweets and the other girl said that she would like thousands of chocolates. The wishes came true but there was one problem, the girls ate lots of sweets that they were too lazy to look after the magical animal. They had a little sleep and they were not lazy anymore but they looked out the window and the animal was gone. They searched everywhere but they couldn't find it. They saw the next-door neighbour and the magical dog was there, they tried to get it but the animal didn't want to go. So they tried their best and finally, it went.

Wioletta Mucha (8)

St Modwen's Catholic Primary School, Burton-On-Trent

The Lonely Girl

Dear Diary,

Today was my first day at school but it wasn't the best day, here's why.

It started off like normal, my parents dropped me to school but when I went inside, it was massive. There were lots of rooms everywhere and then a teacher gave me a piece of paper and it said 'Classroom A1' on it. I went to the classroom and there were lots of children inside, so I sat down at my desk and the teacher said, "You're late on your first day of school, but welcome." Then suddenly the school bell started ringing and it was time for a break. I went outside and I asked someone to play with me but they completely ignored me. Then I realised I wasn't making any new friends, apart from one. I went back to my classroom and after a few hours of learning, I went back home.

Monika Olechowska (9)

St Modwen's Catholic Primary School, Burton-On-Trent

The Myths Of Noodle Land!

Dear Diary,

It's me Libby and at the moment, I am doing my tea party with my friends, Mr Tiddywinkles, Blue, Rabbi, Blanktea and Feathers. We are all just having a tea party outside, it's fun! My teddies and I had no idea that we were going to go on an adventure to Noodle Land.

My teddies and I went on an adventure to Noodle Land. At Noodle Land, there is a land of spaghetti there, OMG it was amazing.

Noodle Land is made of noodles just like in my dream. We saw a tea party stand with cupcakes and all sorts on it. It was amazing.

I loved it and I'm sure the teddies did too. It was time to go home.

Libby Clarke (8)
St Modwen's Catholic Primary School, Burton-On-Trent

YoungWriters®
Est. 1991

Young Writers Information

We hope you have enjoyed reading this book – and that you will continue to in the coming years.

If you're a young writer who enjoys reading and creative writing, or the parent of an enthusiastic poet or story writer, do visit our website **www.youngwriters.co.uk**. Here you will find free competitions, workshops and games, as well as recommended reads, a poetry glossary and our blog. There's lots to keep budding writers motivated to write!

If you would like to order further copies of this book, or any of our other titles, then please give us a call or order via your online account.

Young Writers
Remus House
Coltsfoot Drive
Peterborough
PE2 9BF
(01733) 890066
info@youngwriters.co.uk

Join in the conversation!
Tips, news, giveaways and much more!

f YoungWritersUK   **🐦** @YoungWritersCW